Codex Venereorum Abstracta

Mark Humes

ISBN:1542340926
ISBN-13: 978-1542340922

DEDICATION

For all those who seek the expressions of art and would turn pain into beauty.

ACKNOWLEDGMENTS

A special thank you to Penthouse Magazine for all of the wonderful muses they have introduced me to that inspired the creation of this book. Everyone of these women featured in this book deserve to be immortalized in art and print for all time and I have personally taken this matter to task with this art series and this book.

Naomi Woods

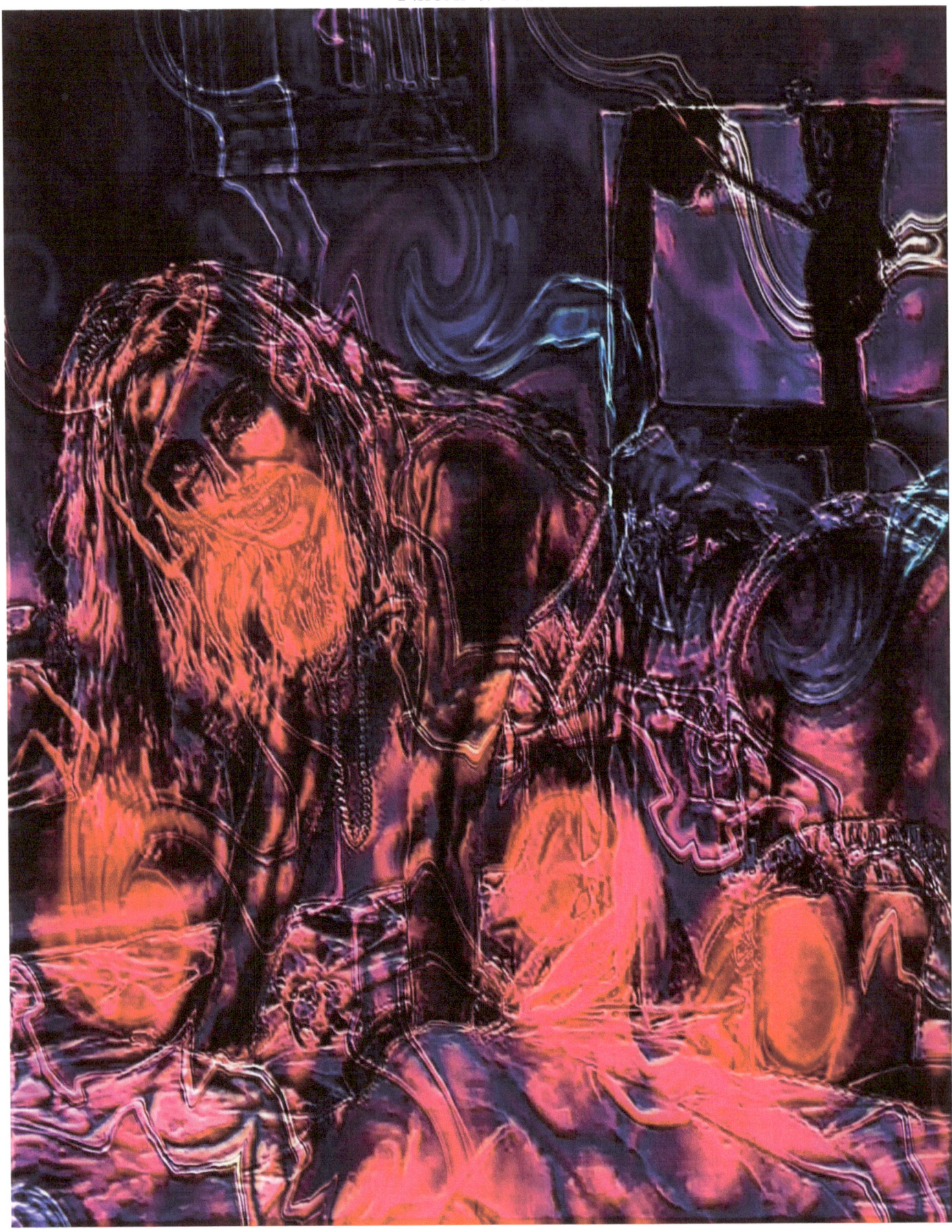

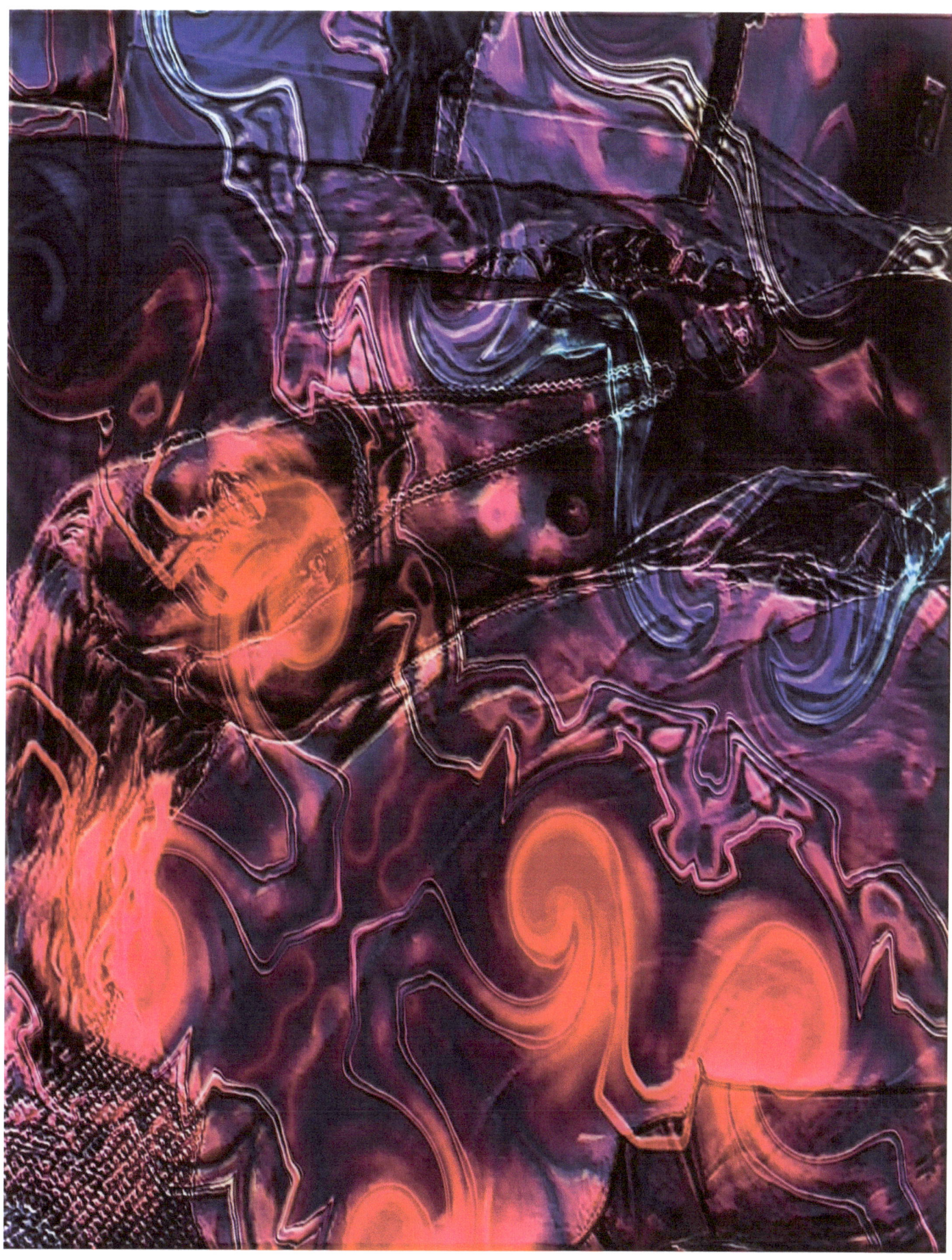

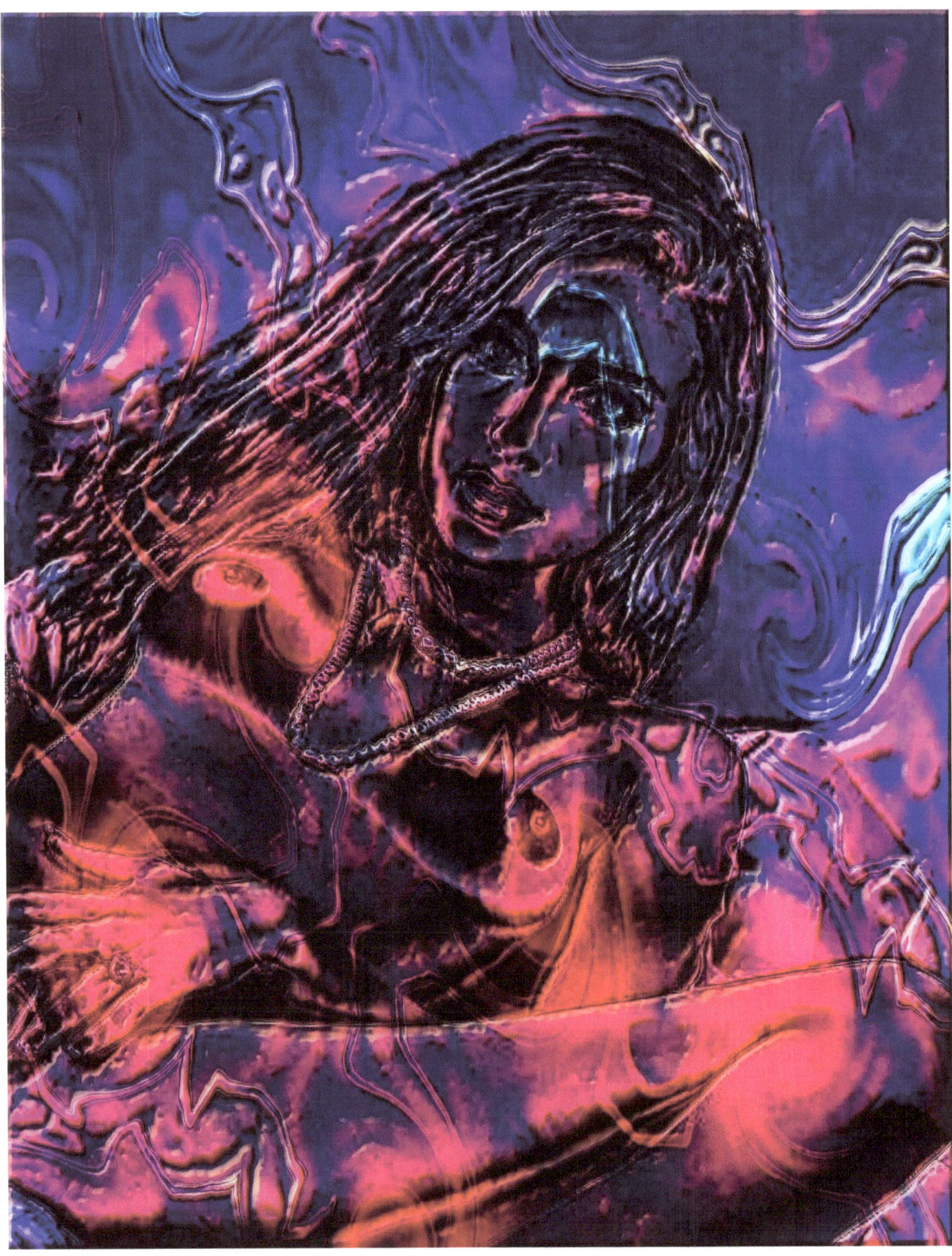

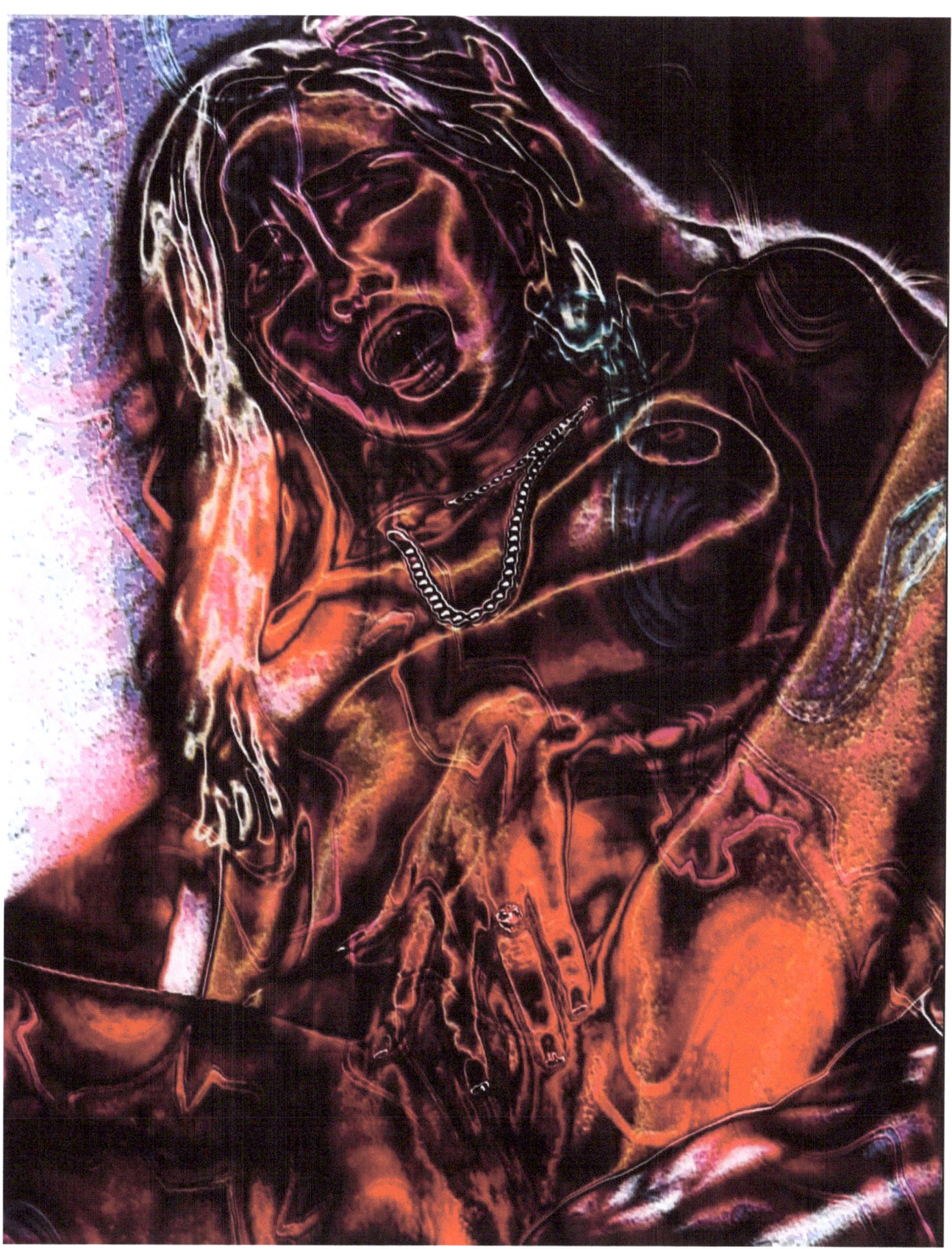

BLAKE

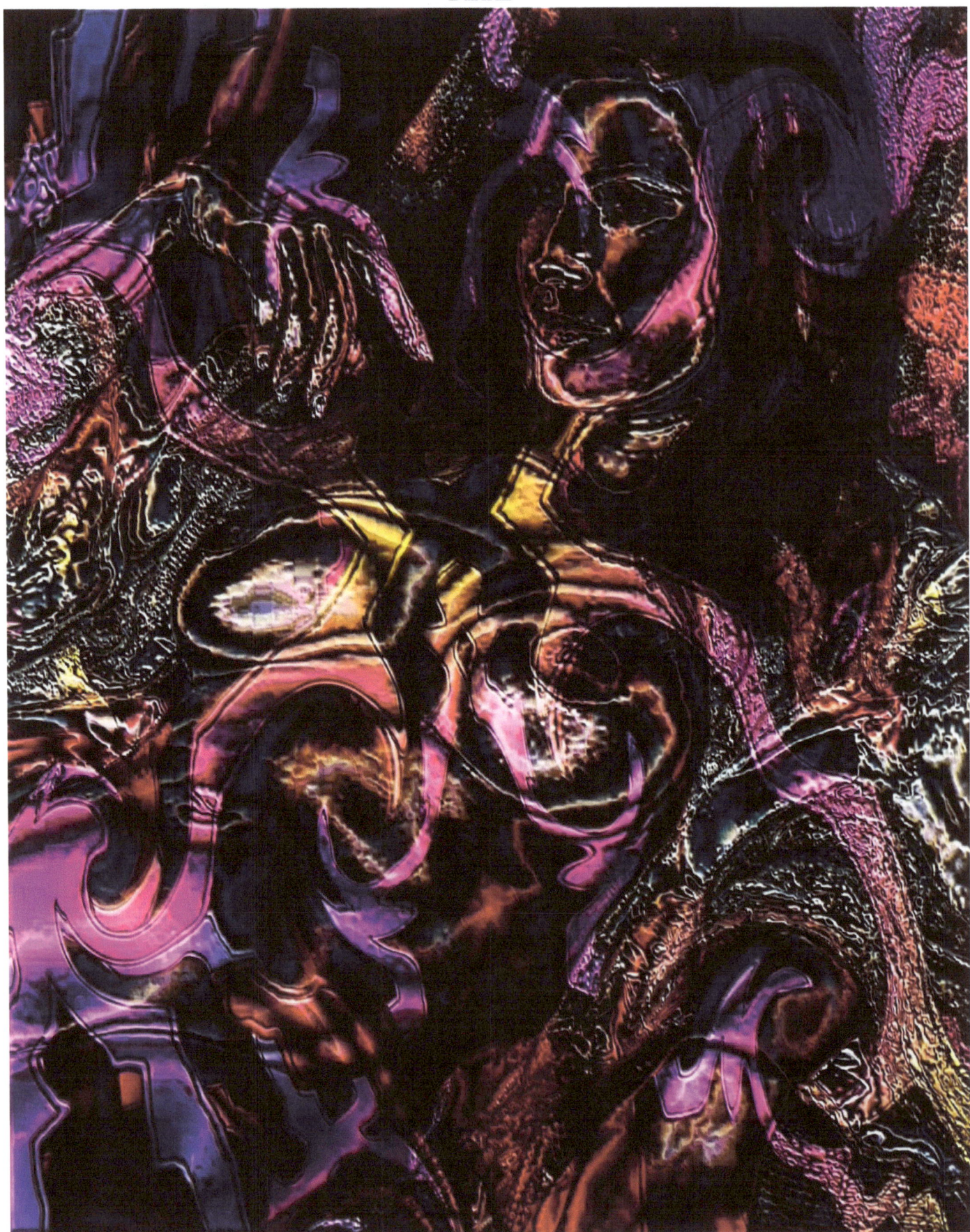

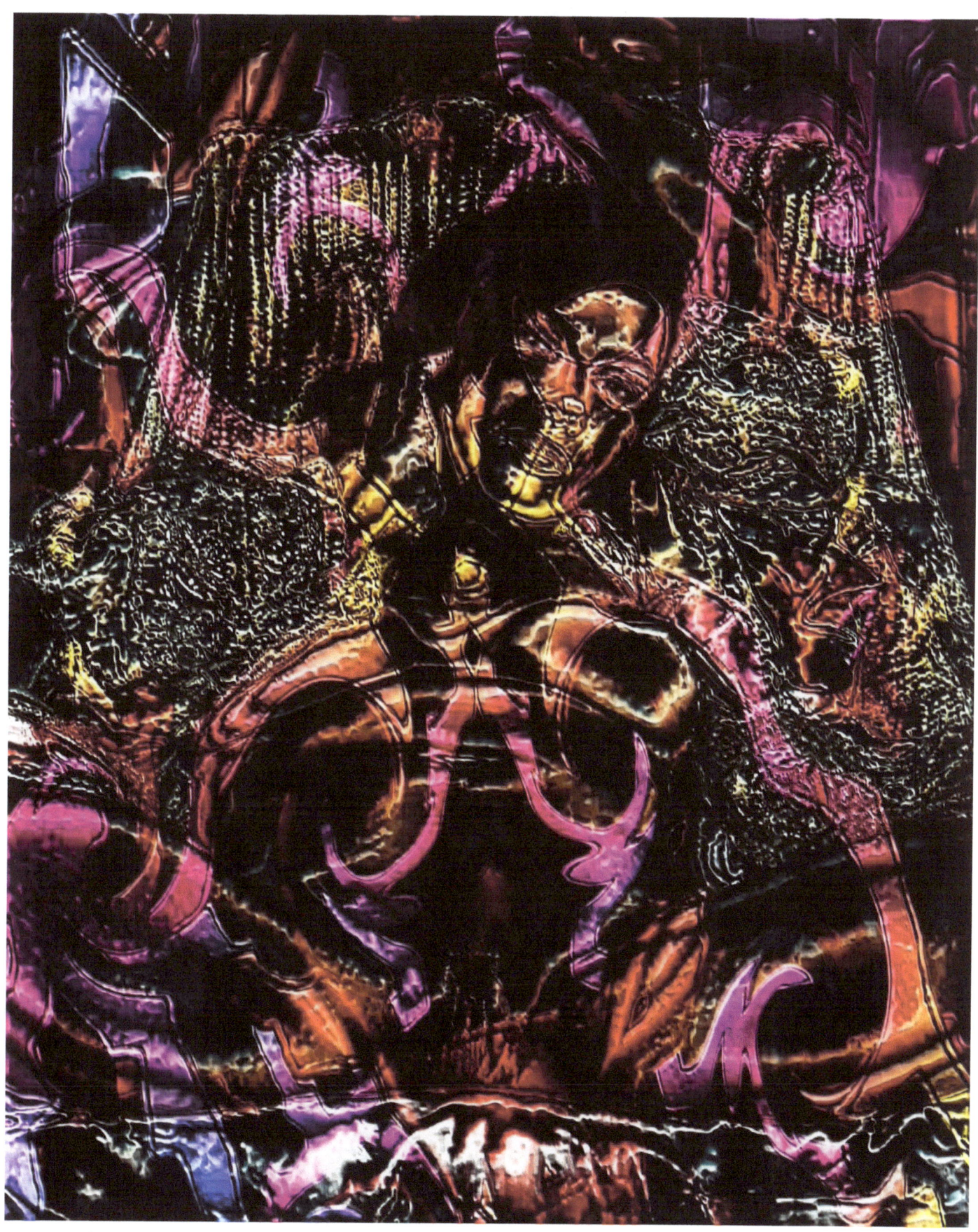

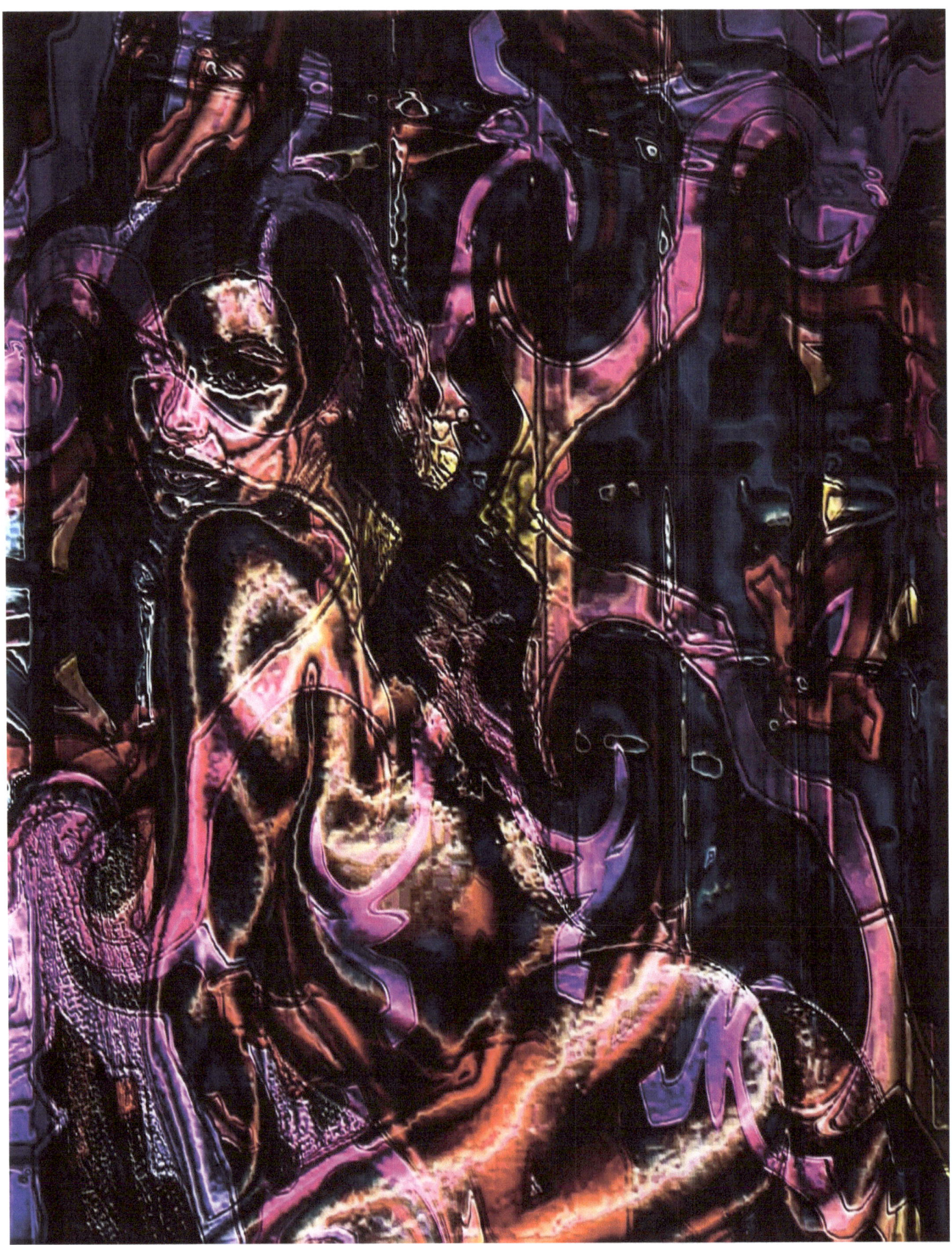

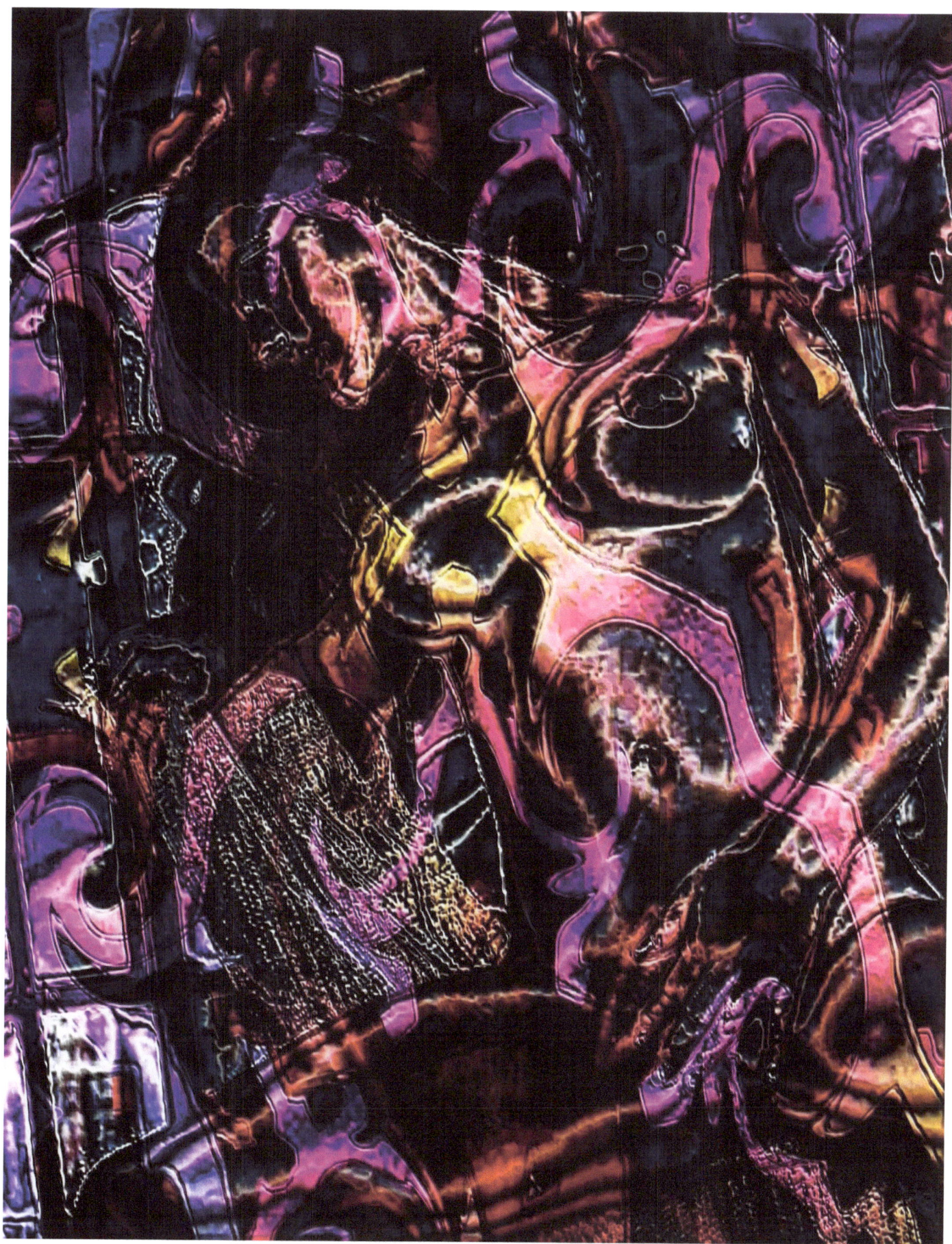

MARY MOODY

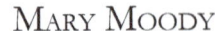

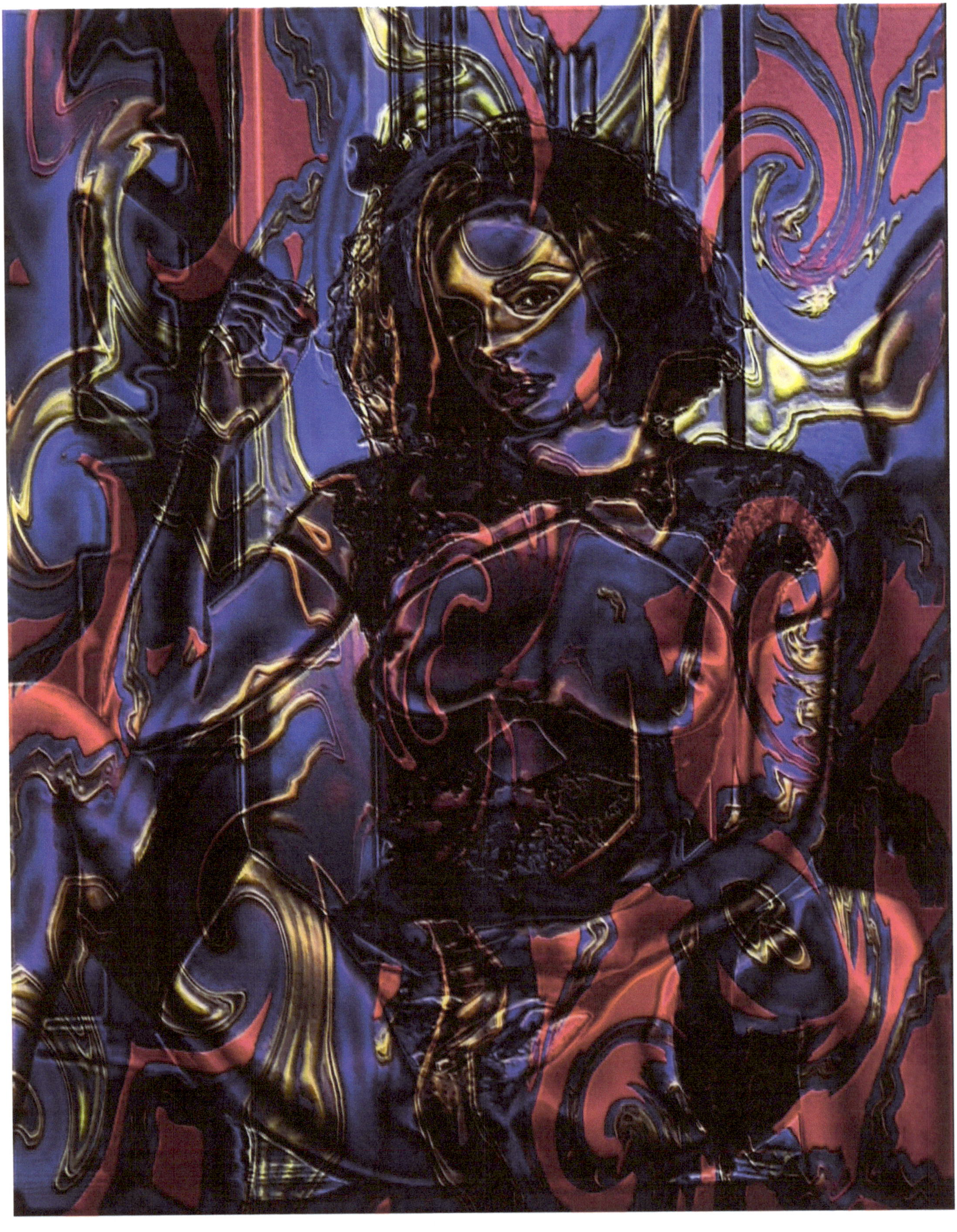

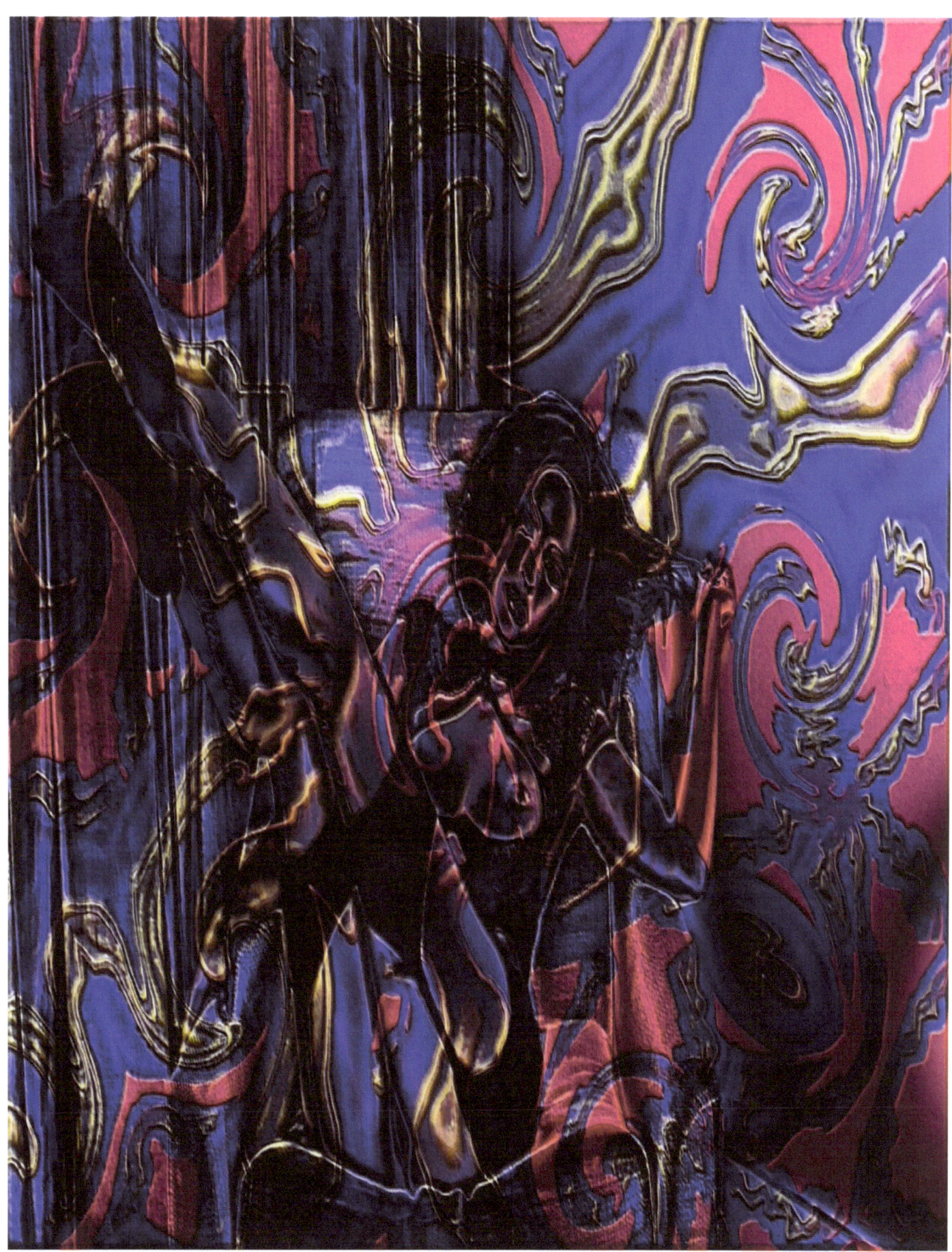

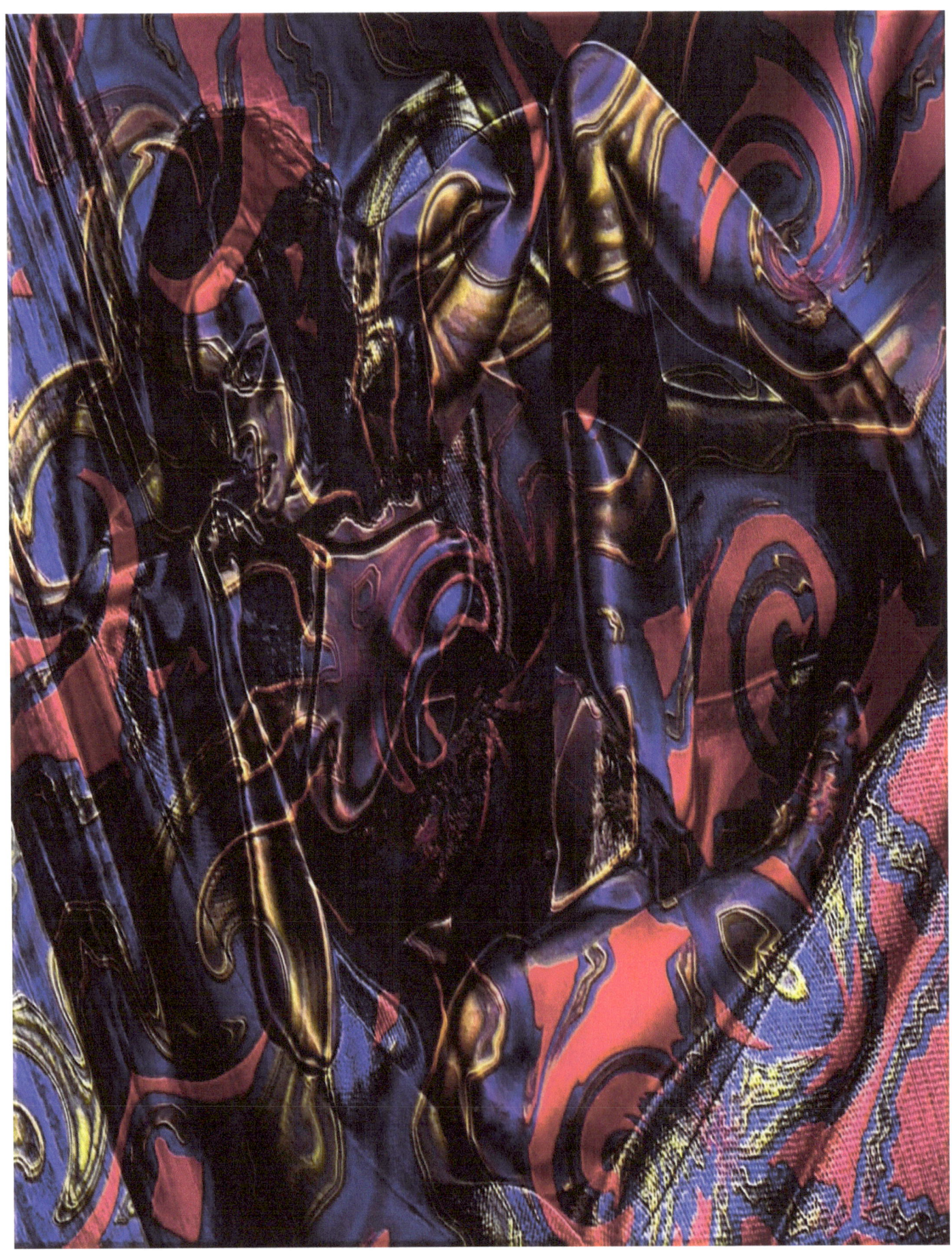

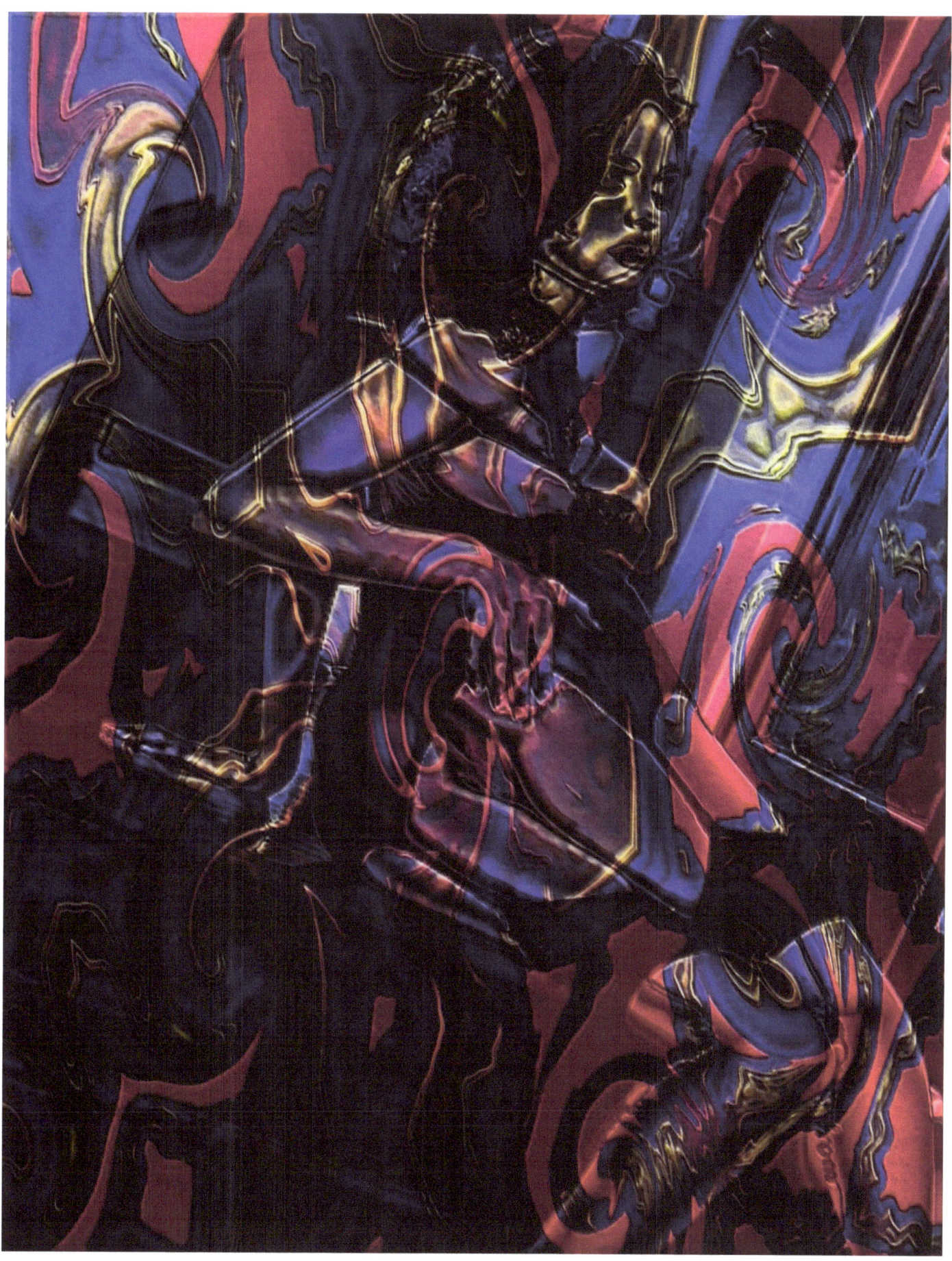

Codex Venereorum Abstracta

MIA MALKOVA

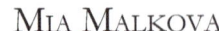

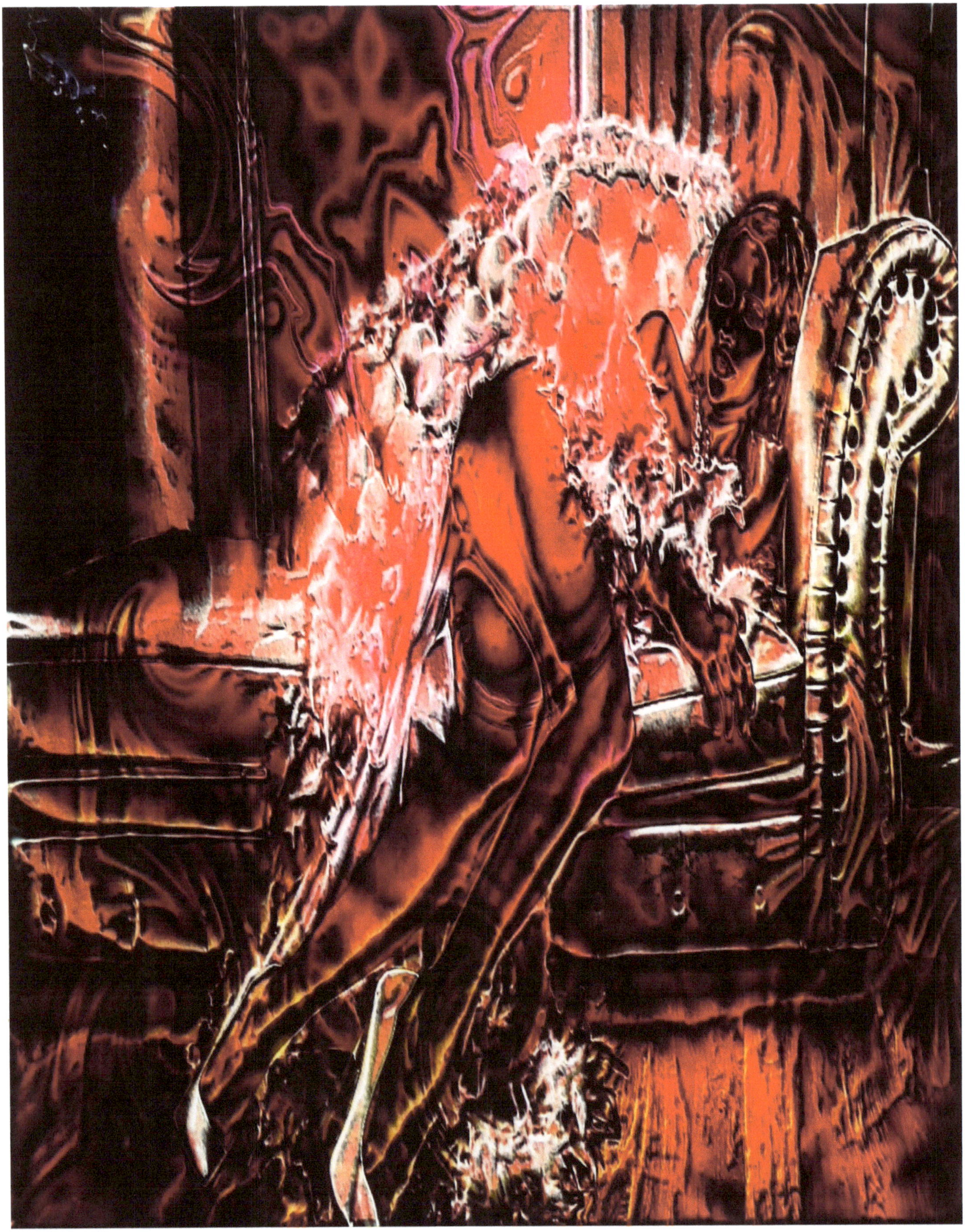

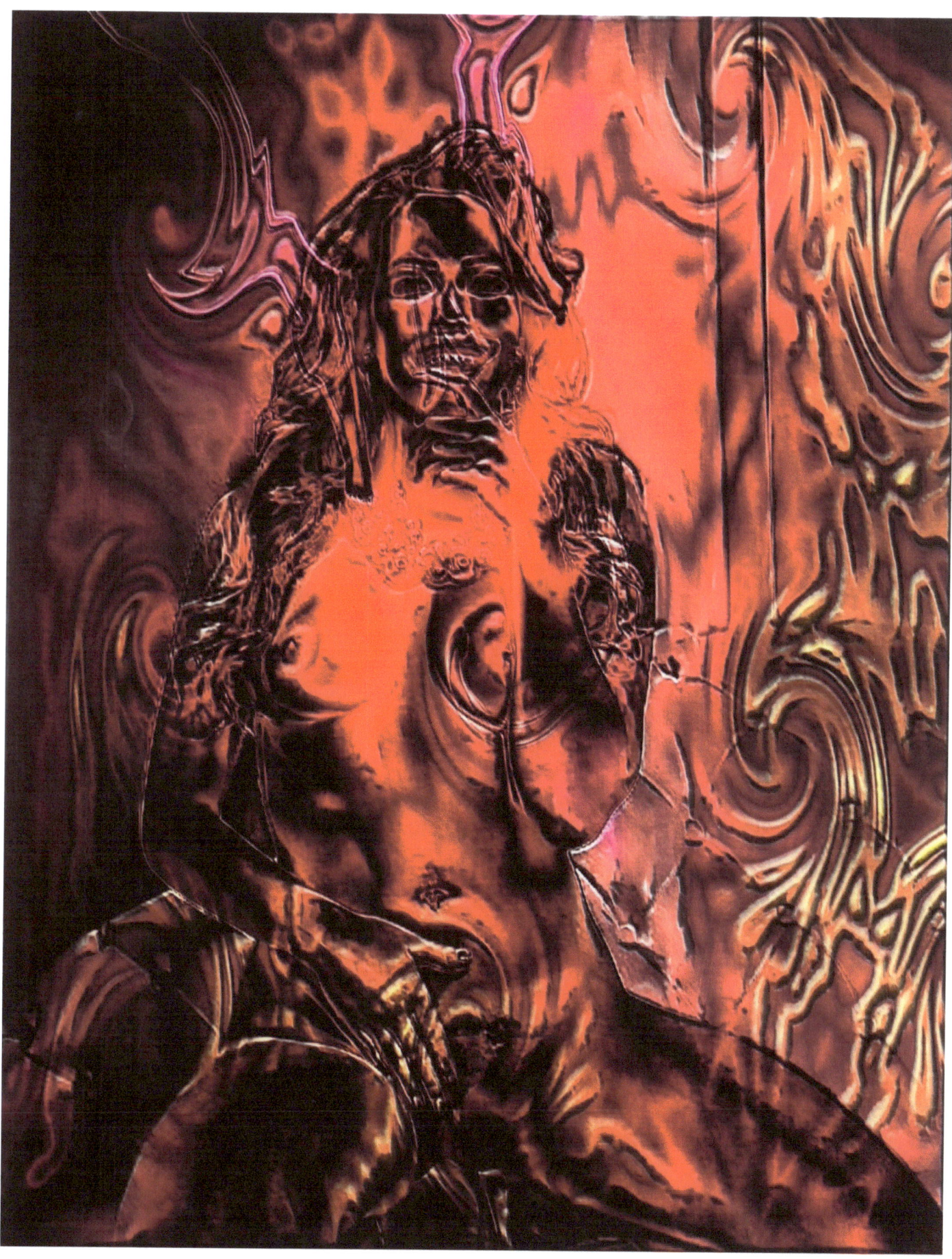

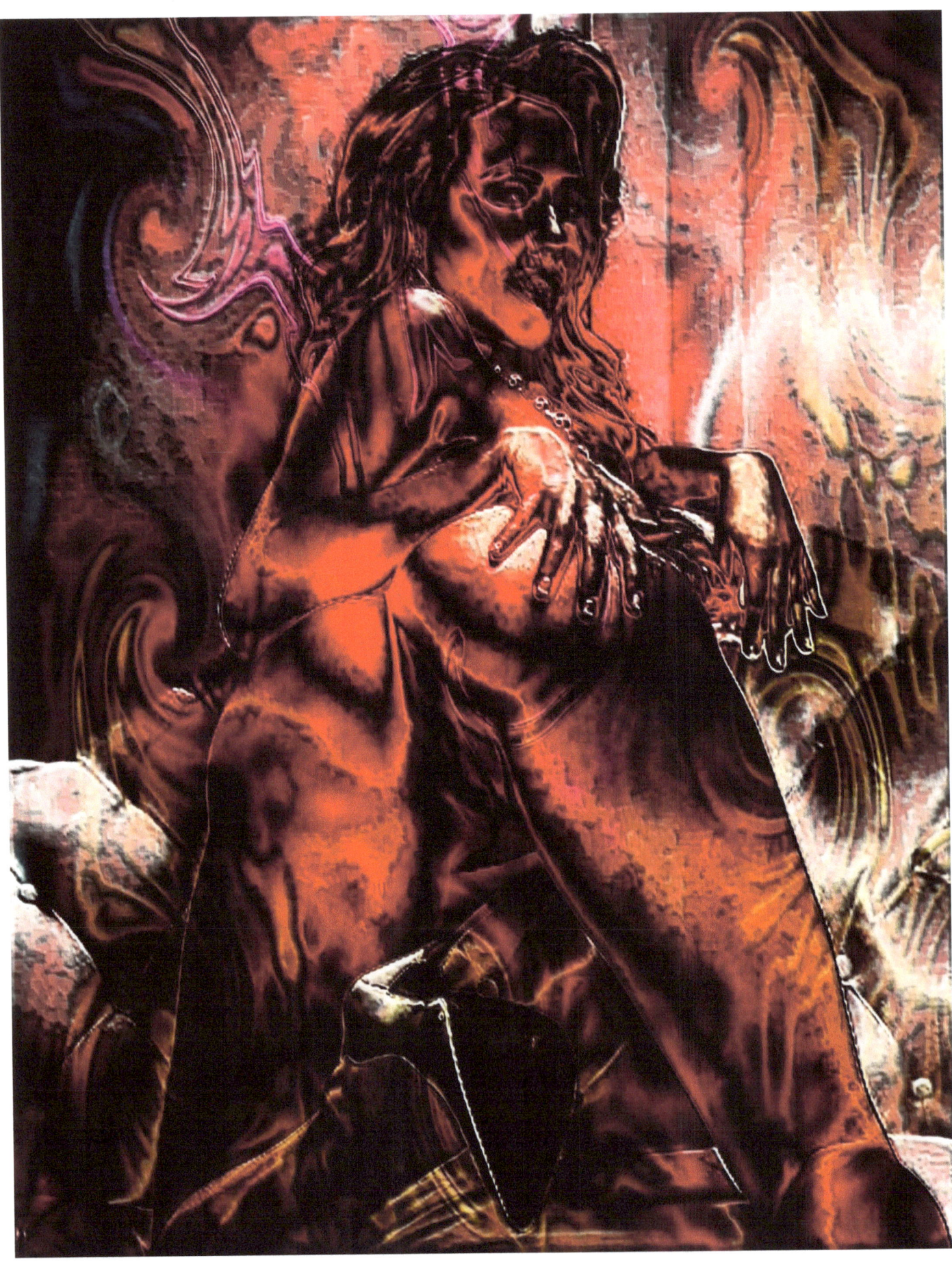

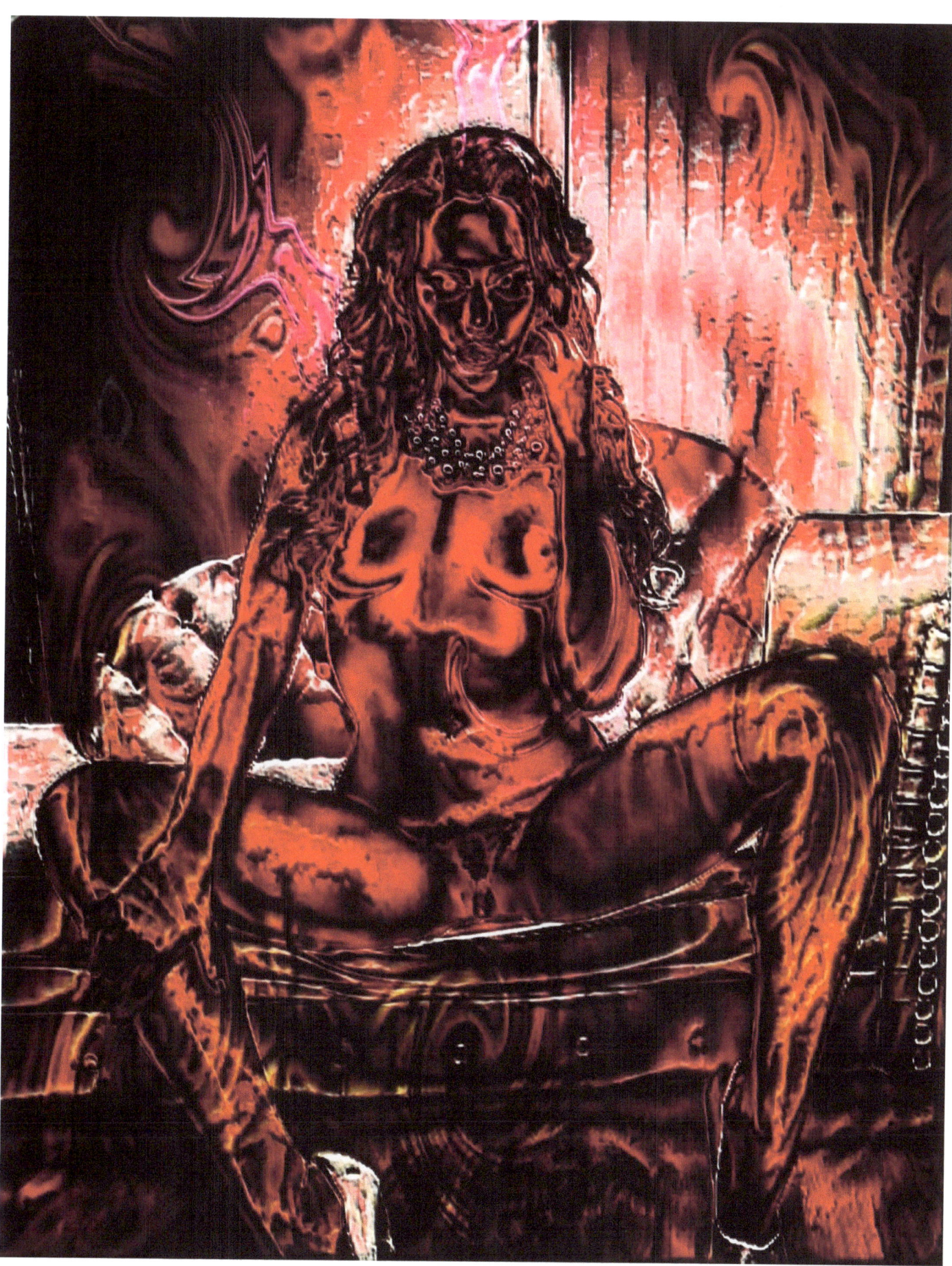

Misty Lovelace

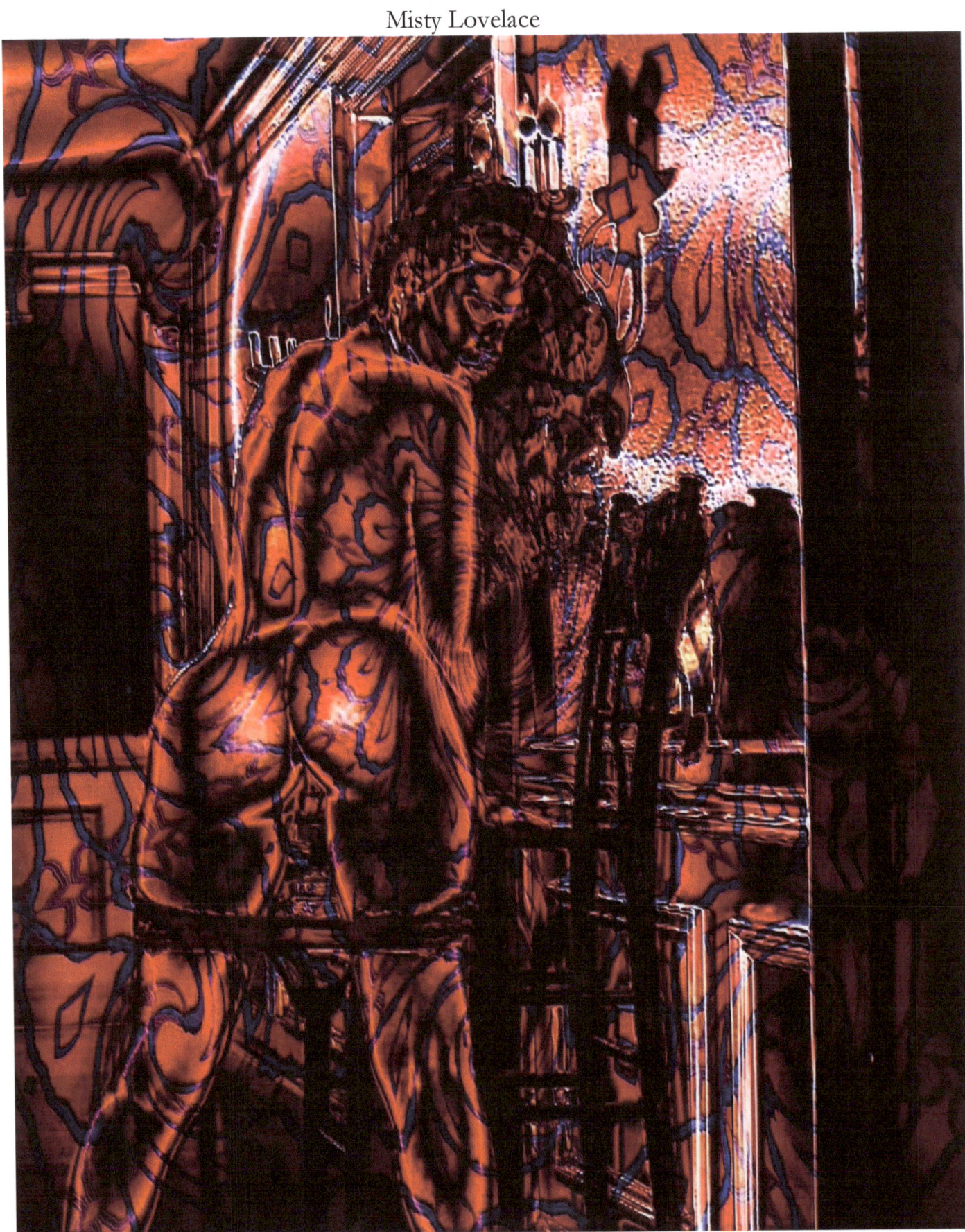

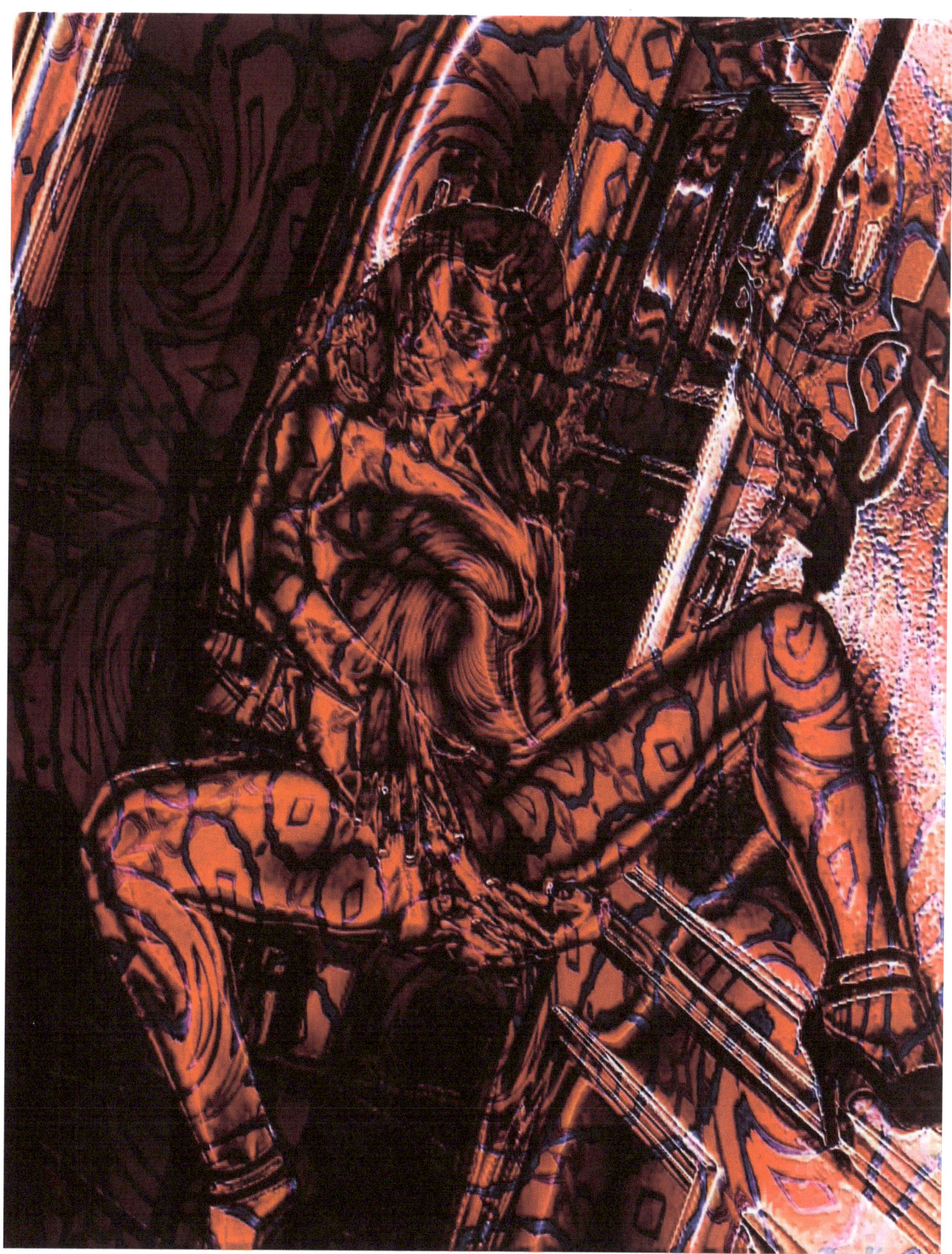

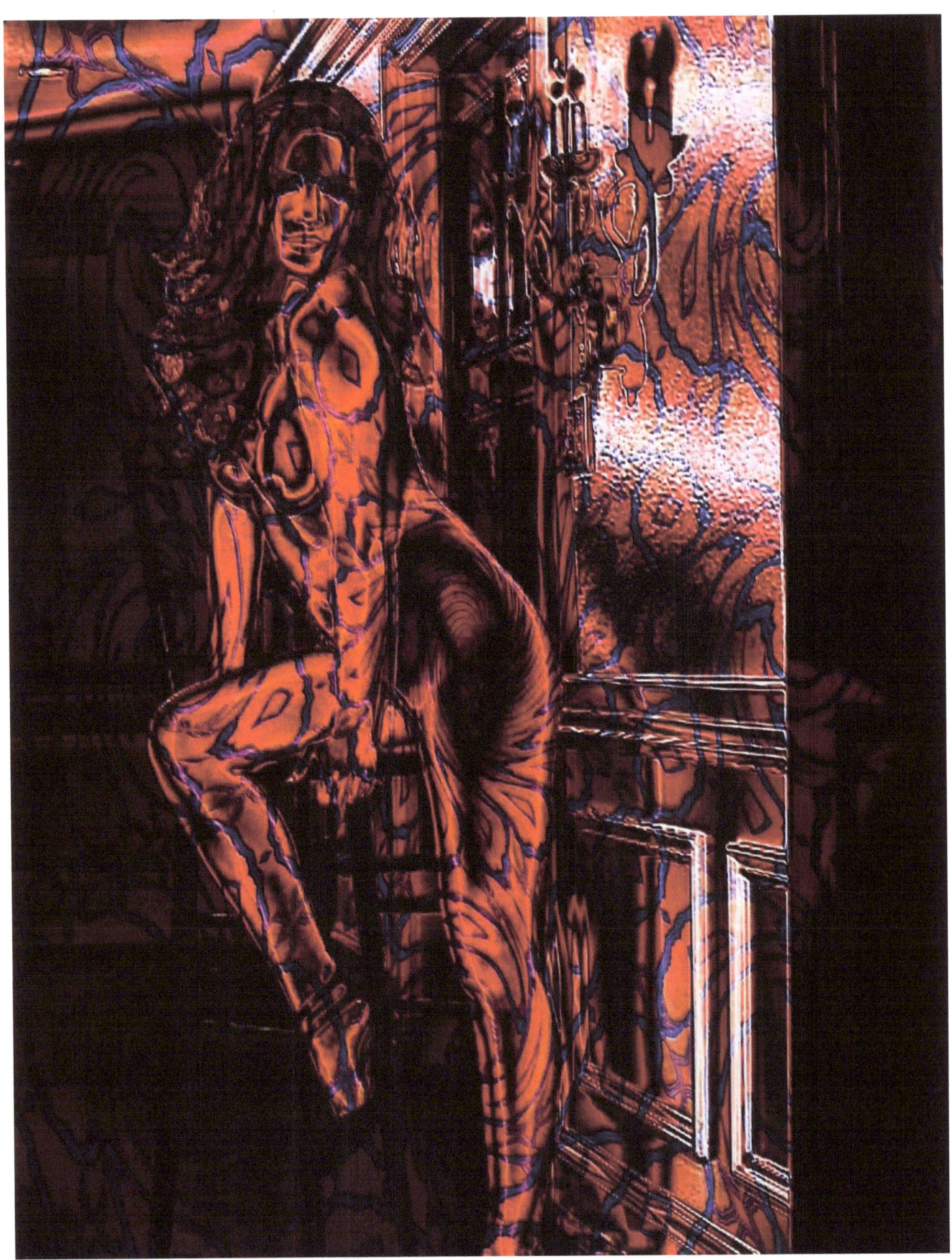

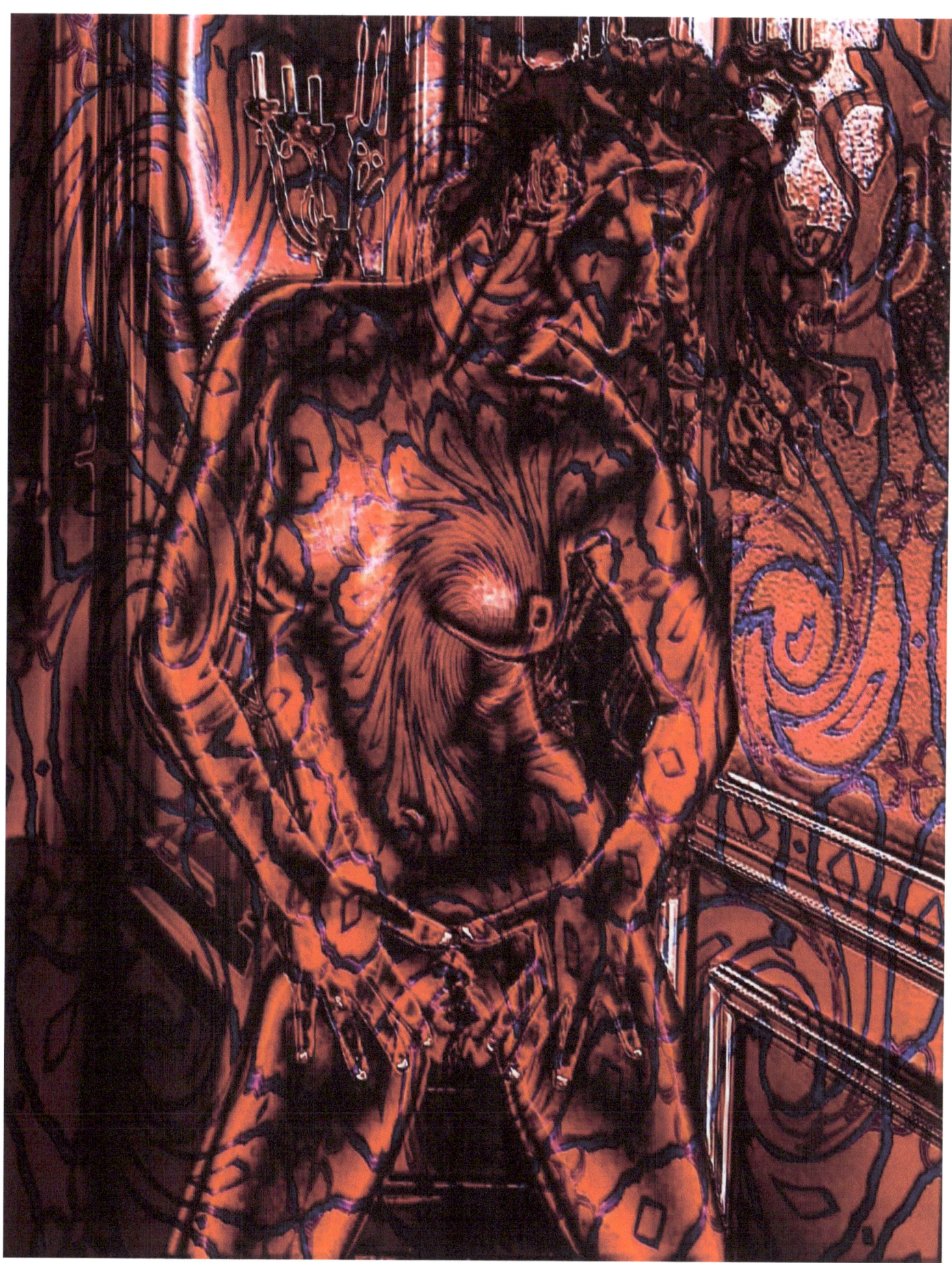

LANA RHOADES

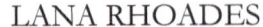

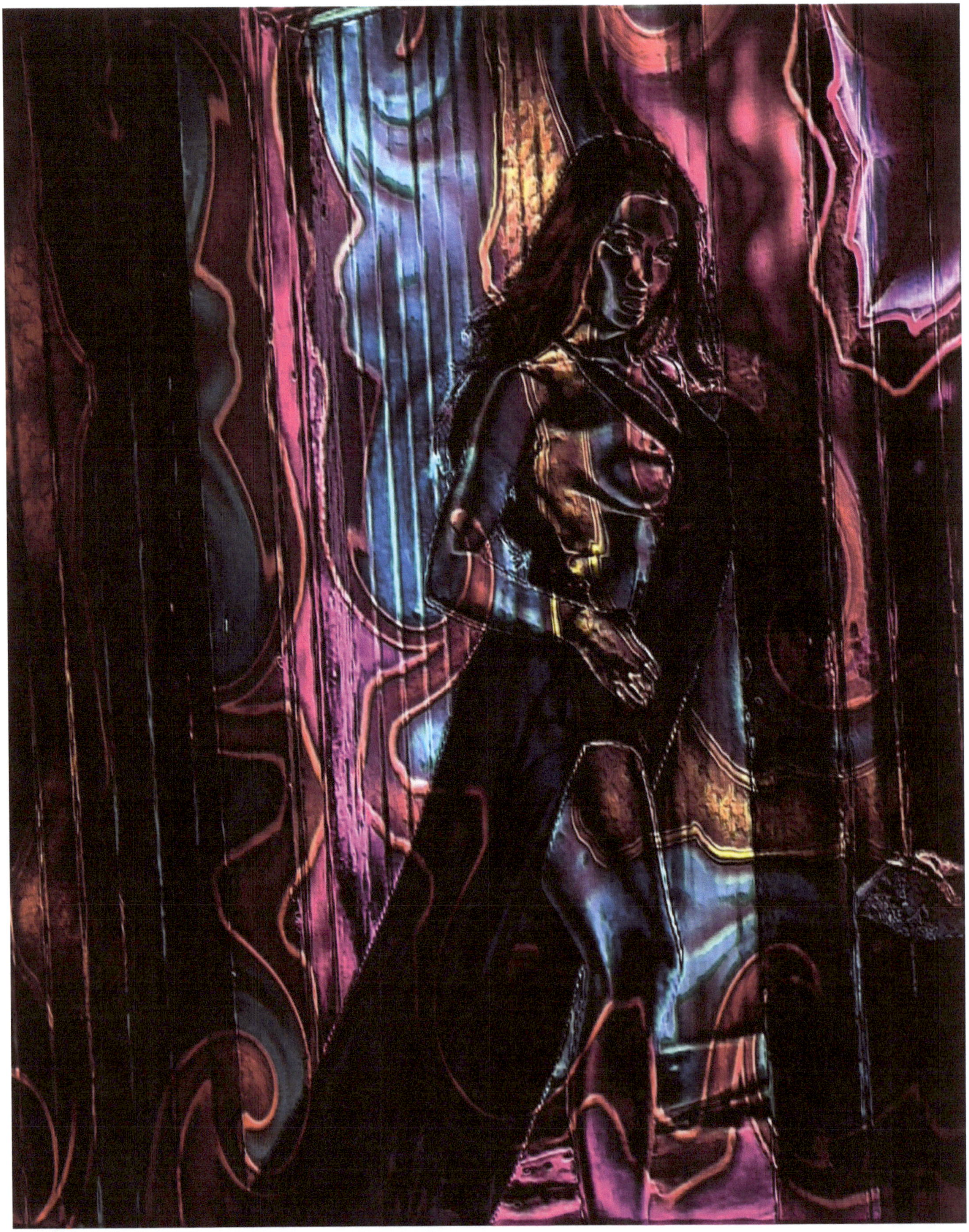

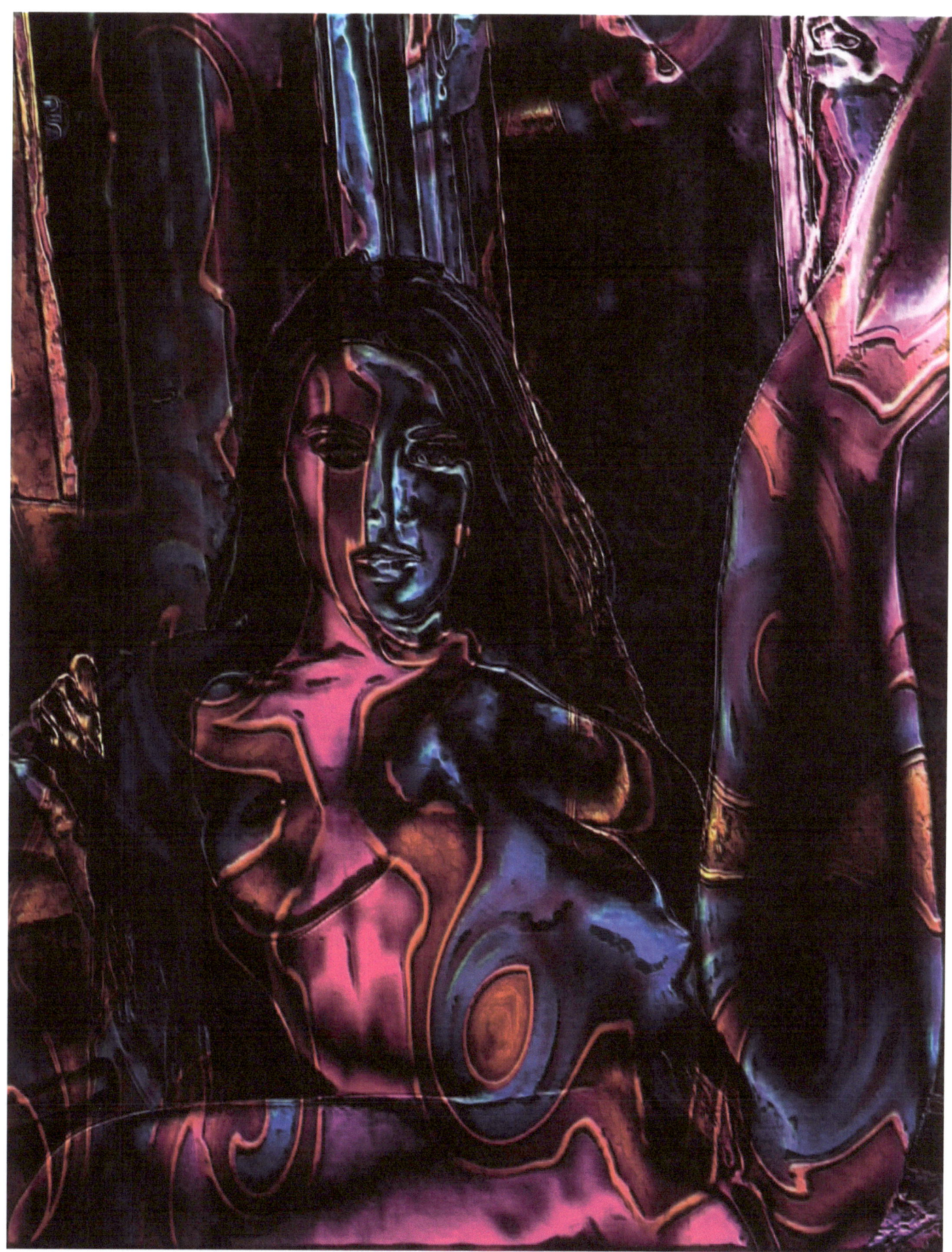

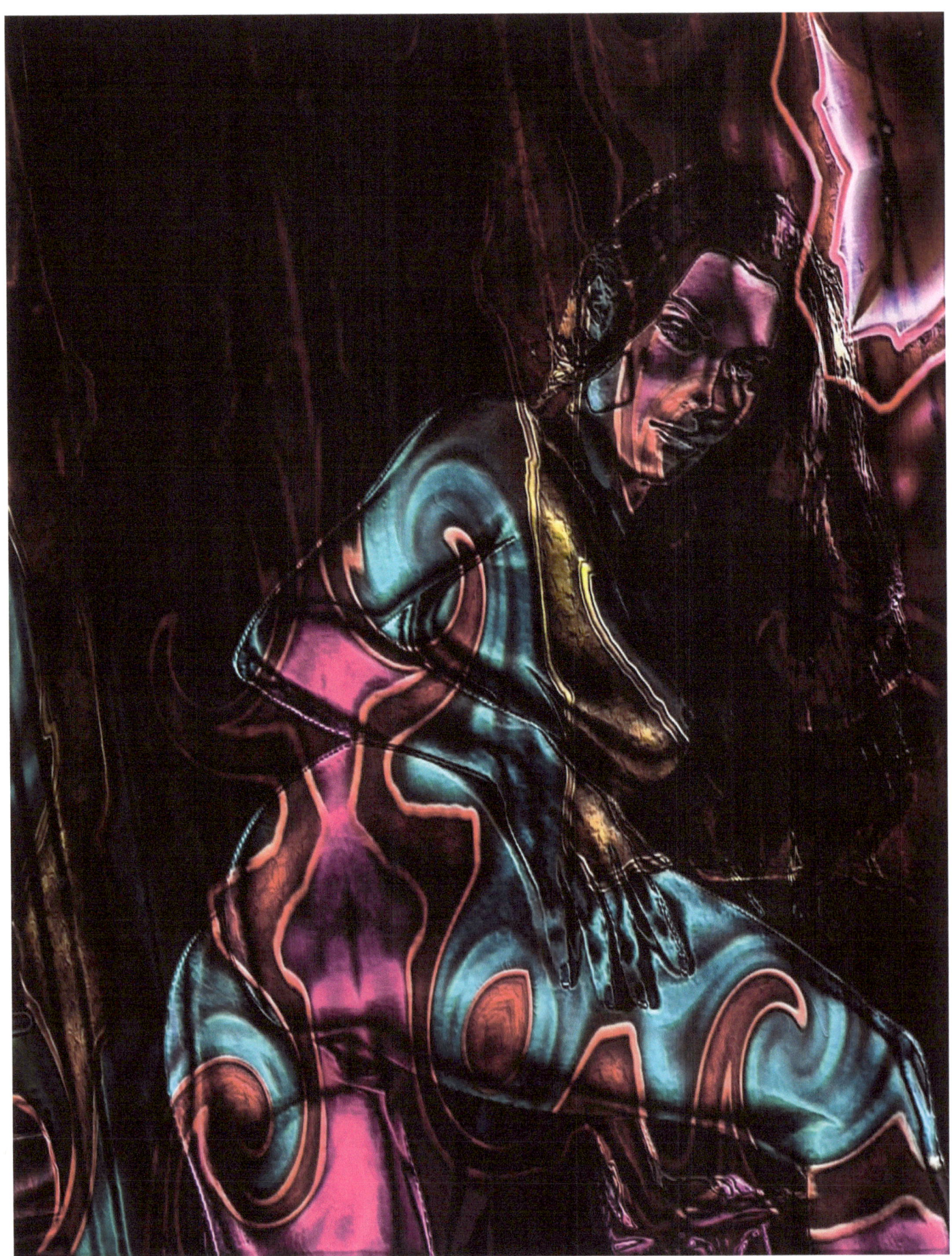

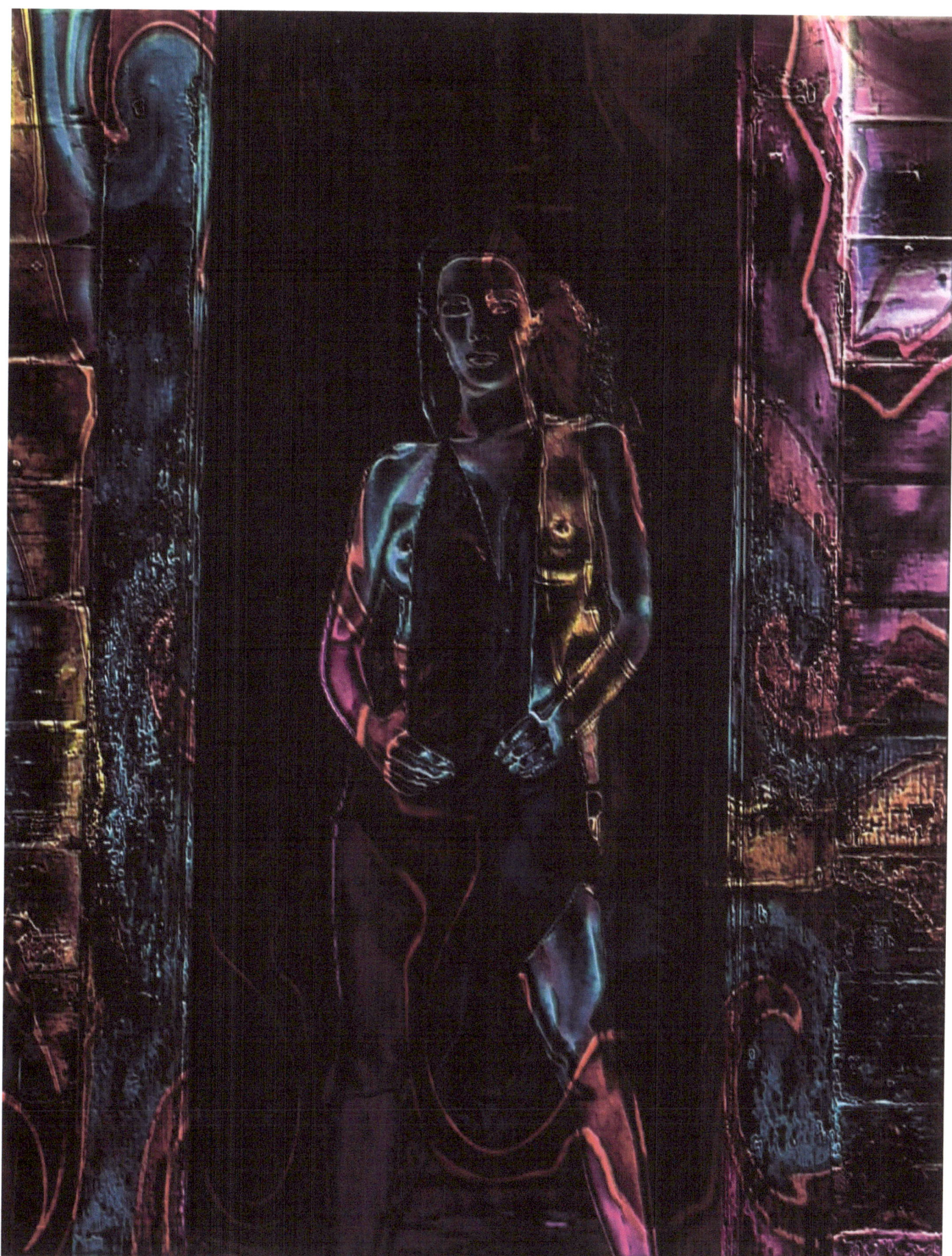

NOELLE MONIQUE

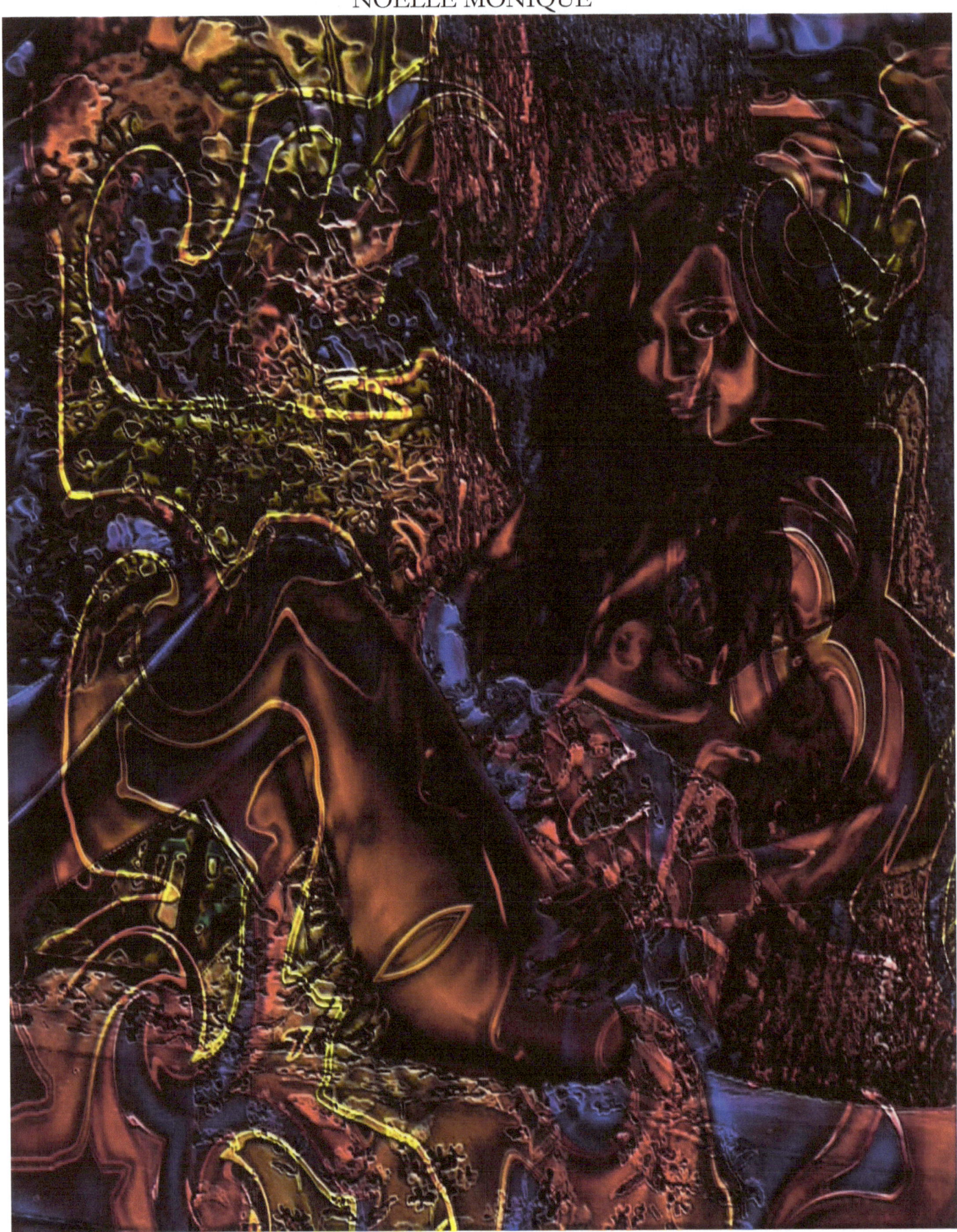

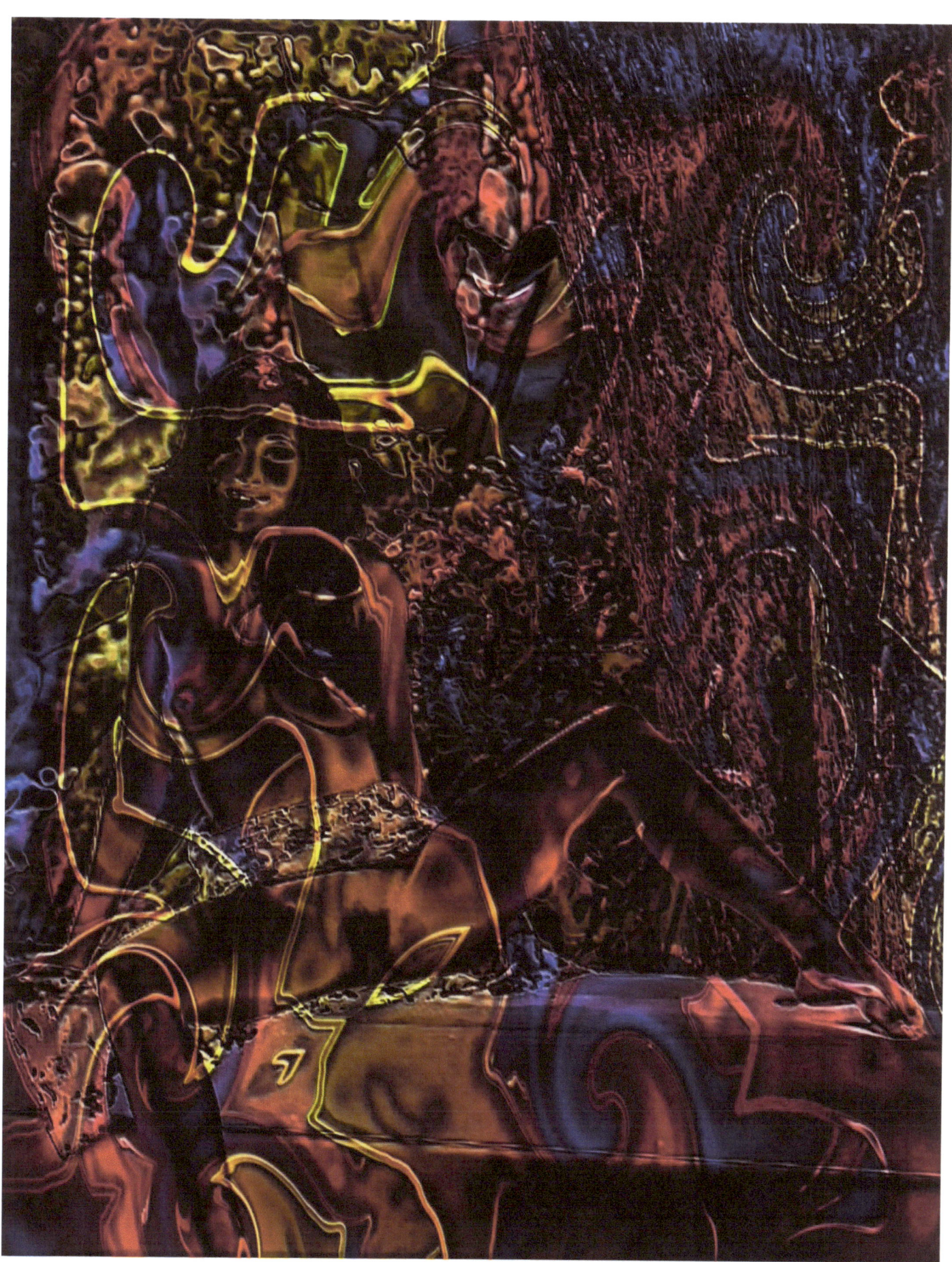

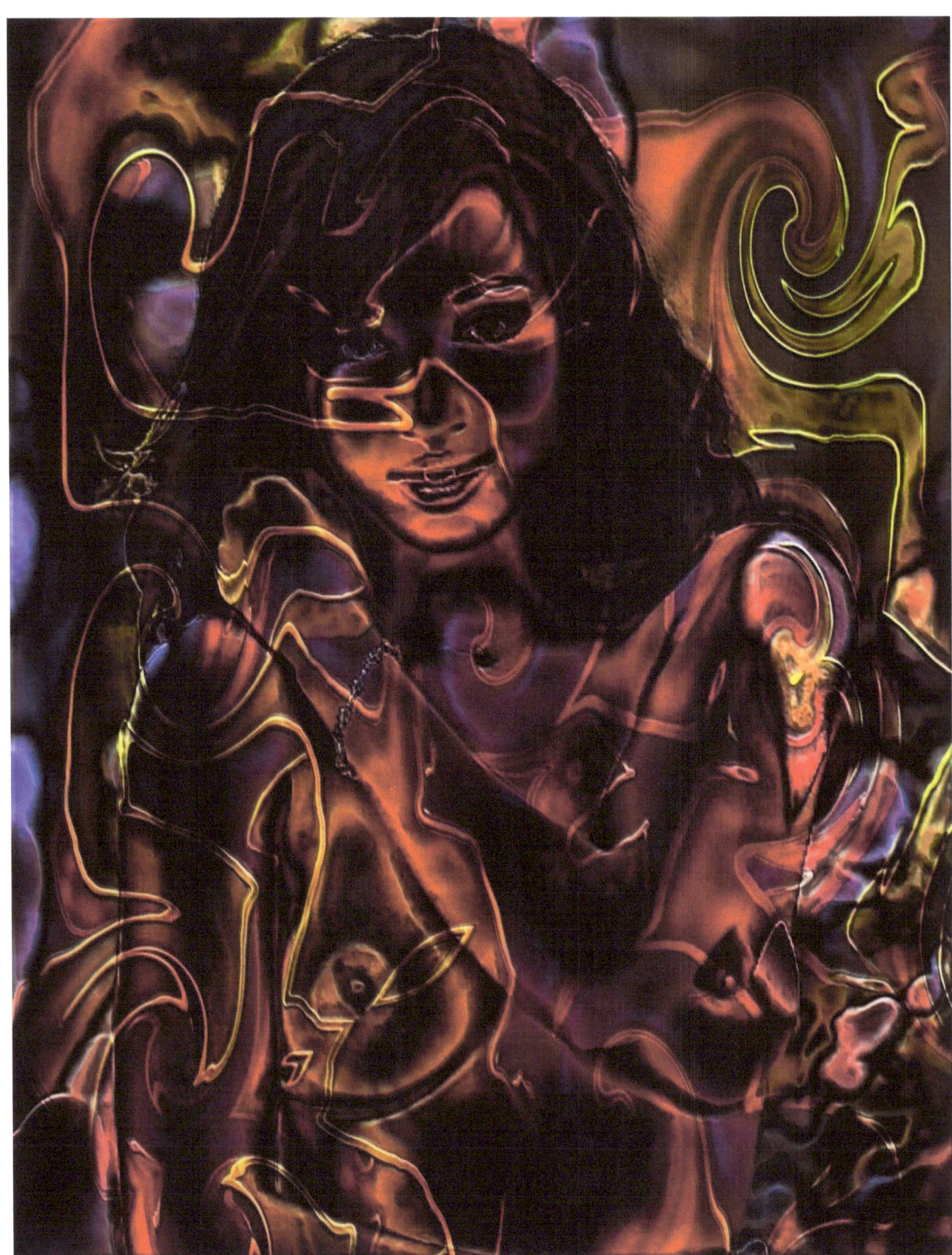

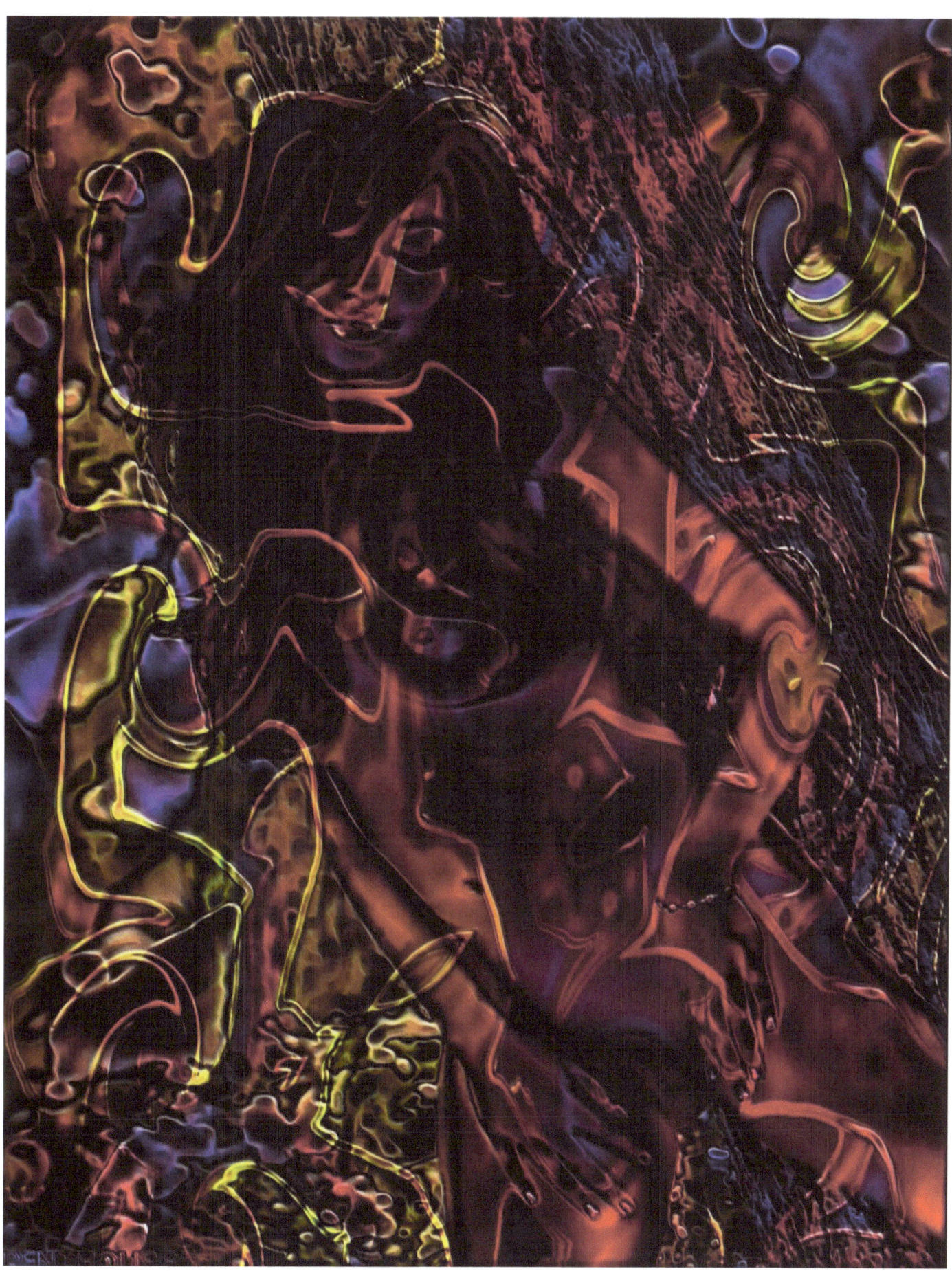

LILY IVY

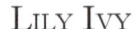

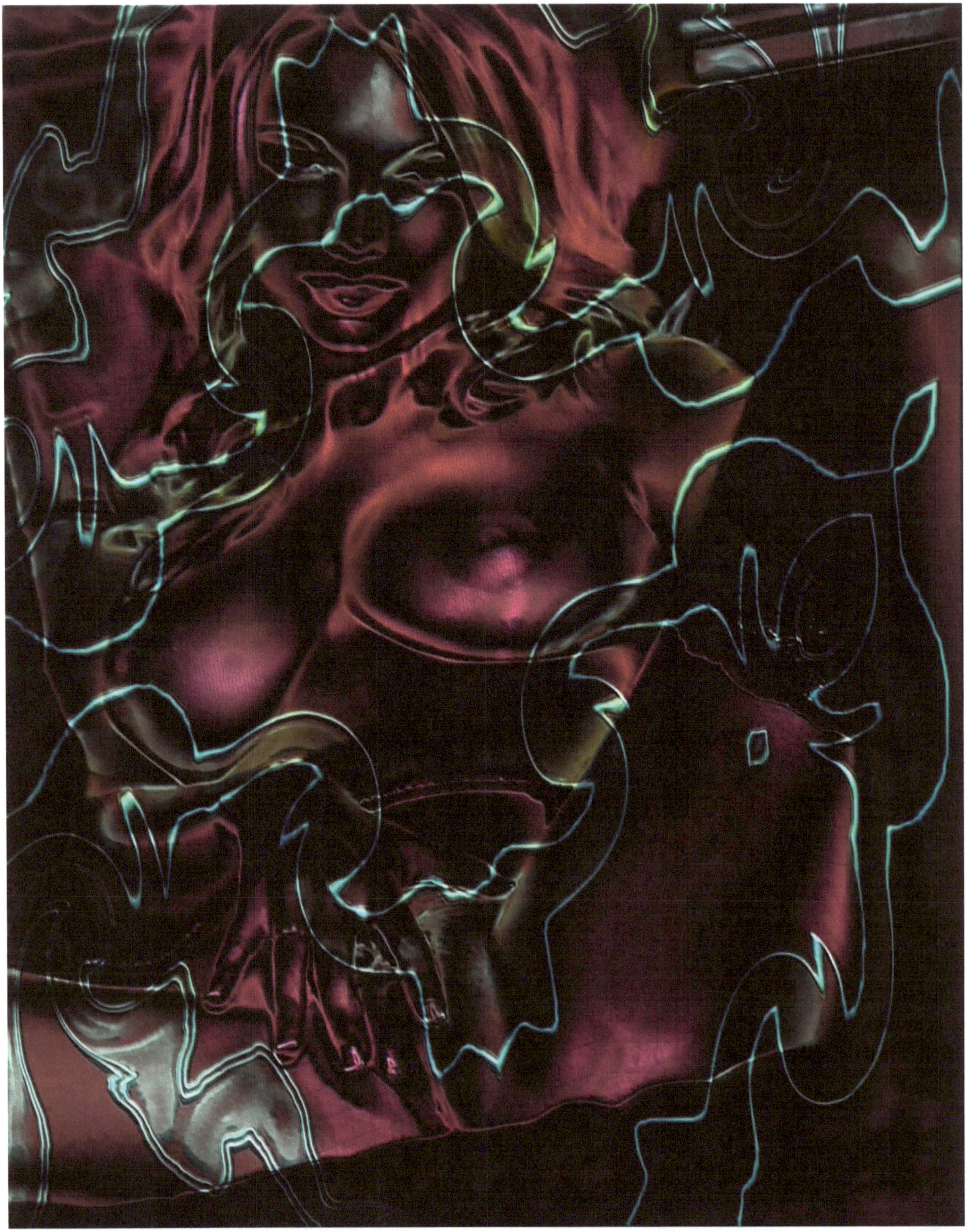

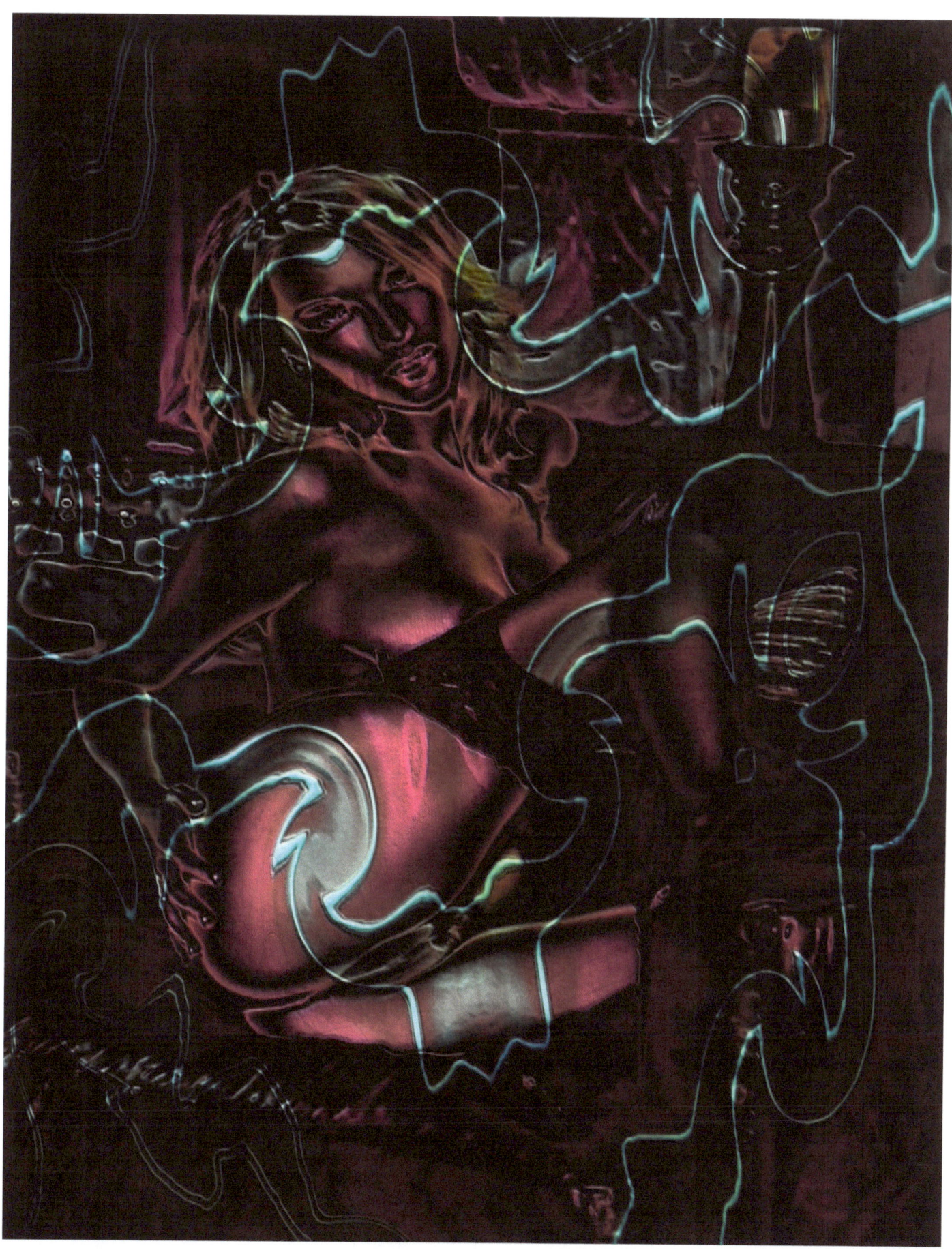

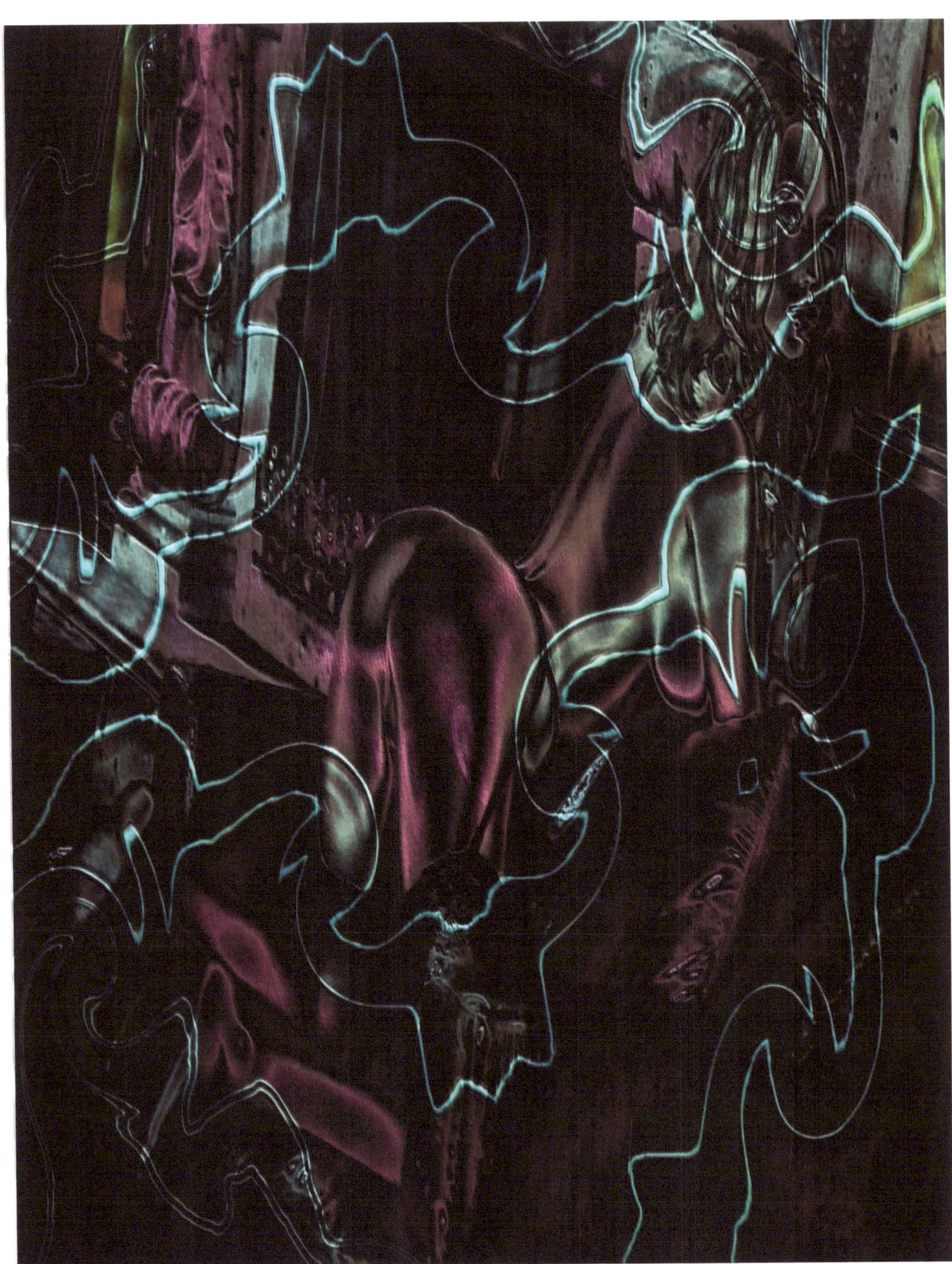

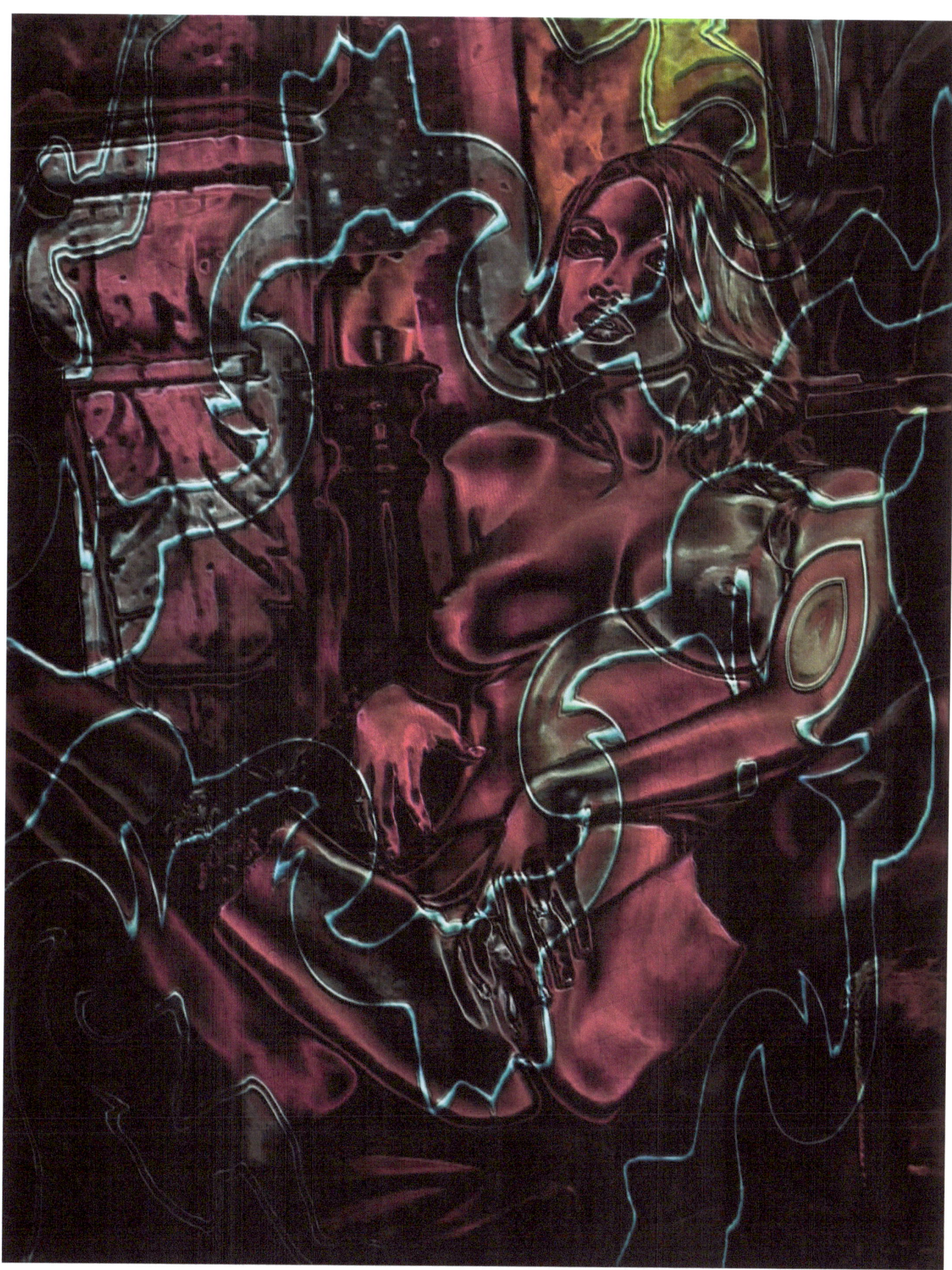

PAULINI

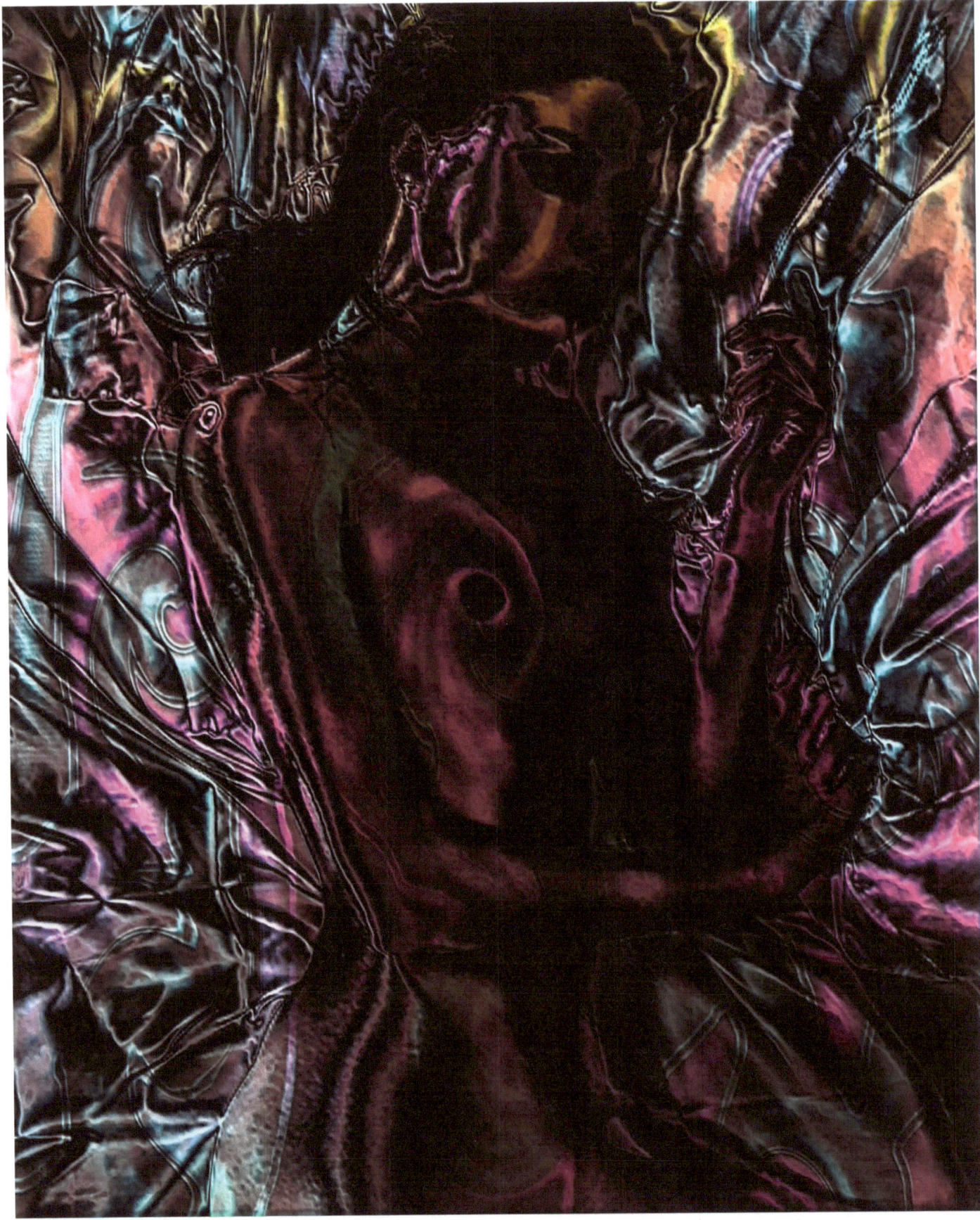

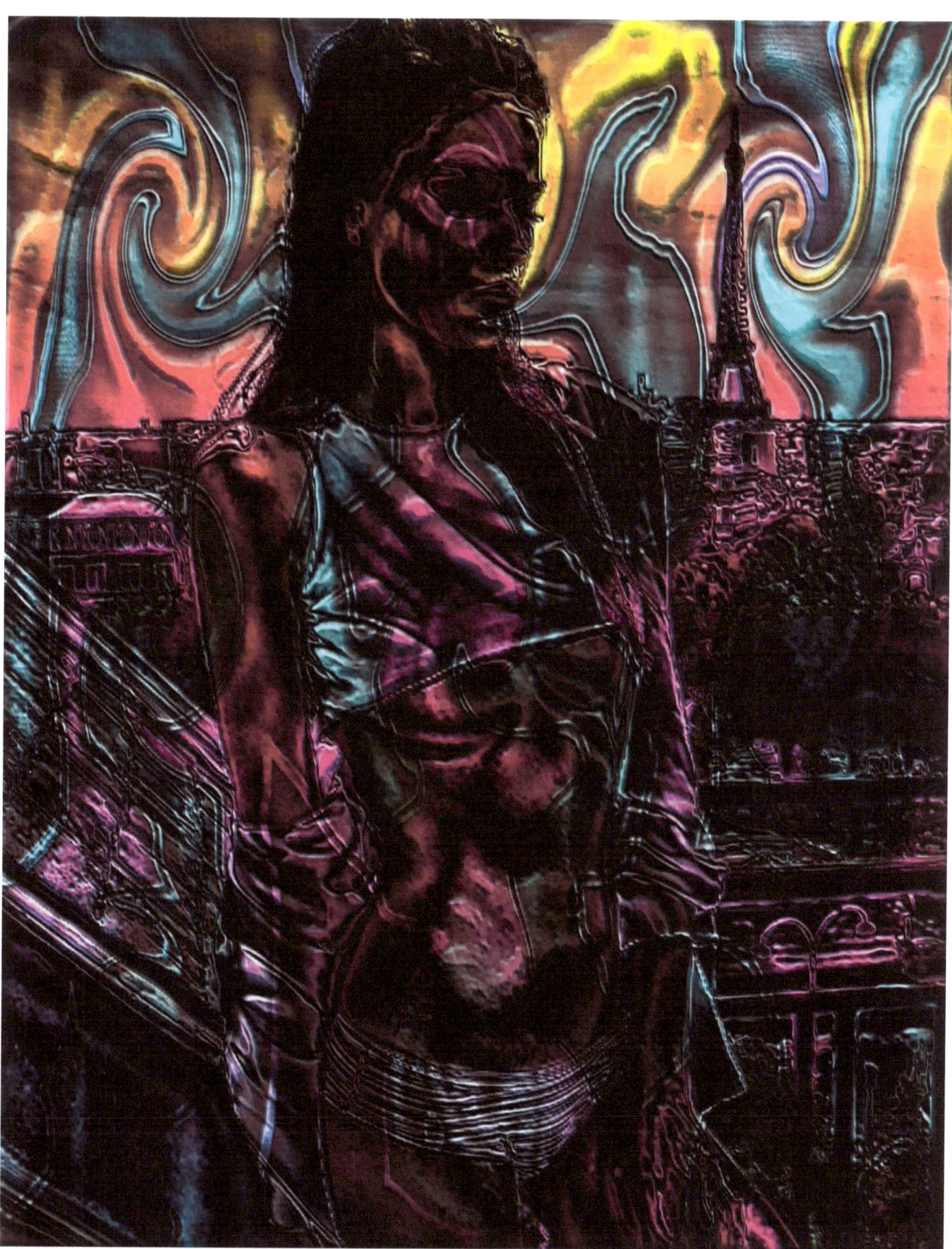

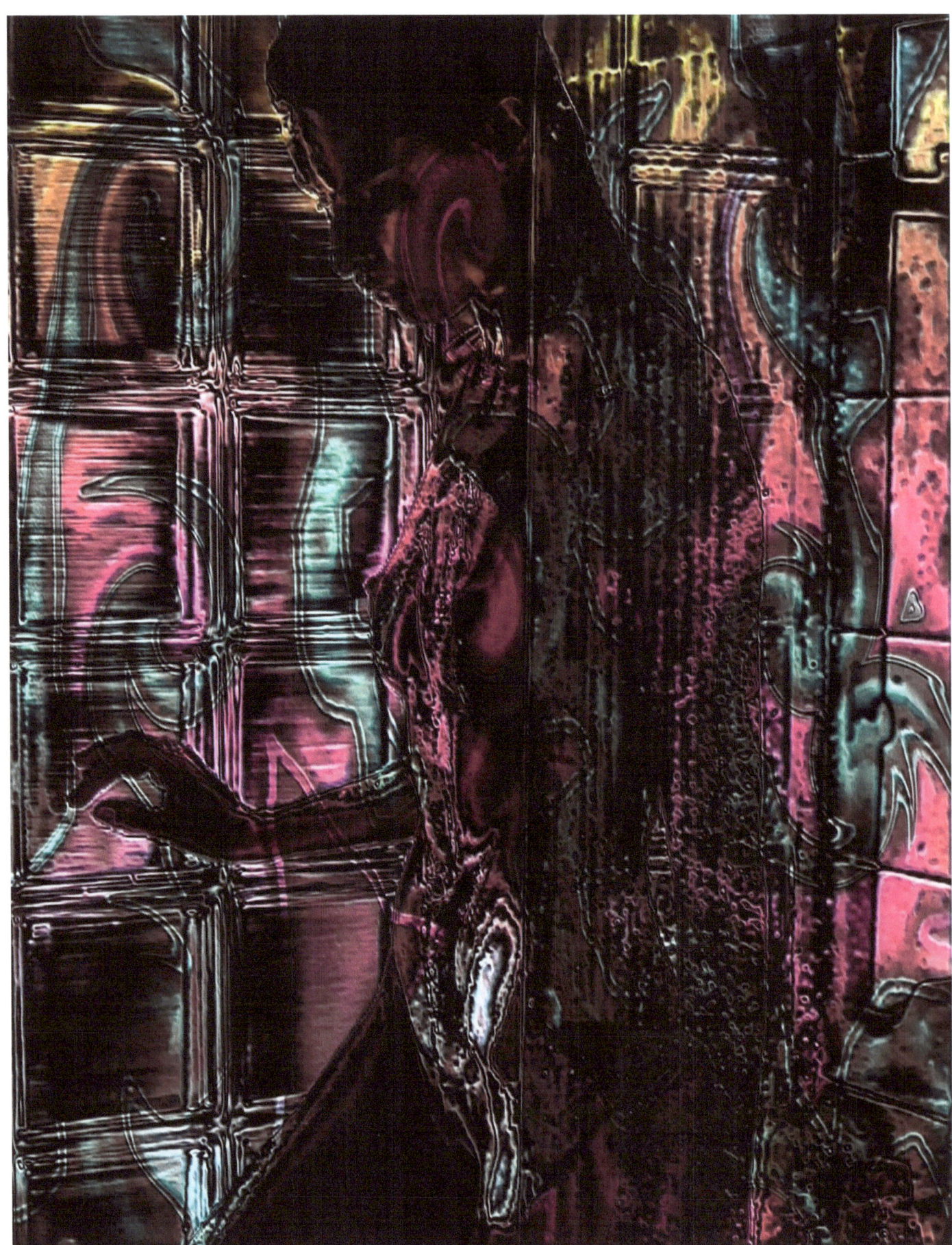

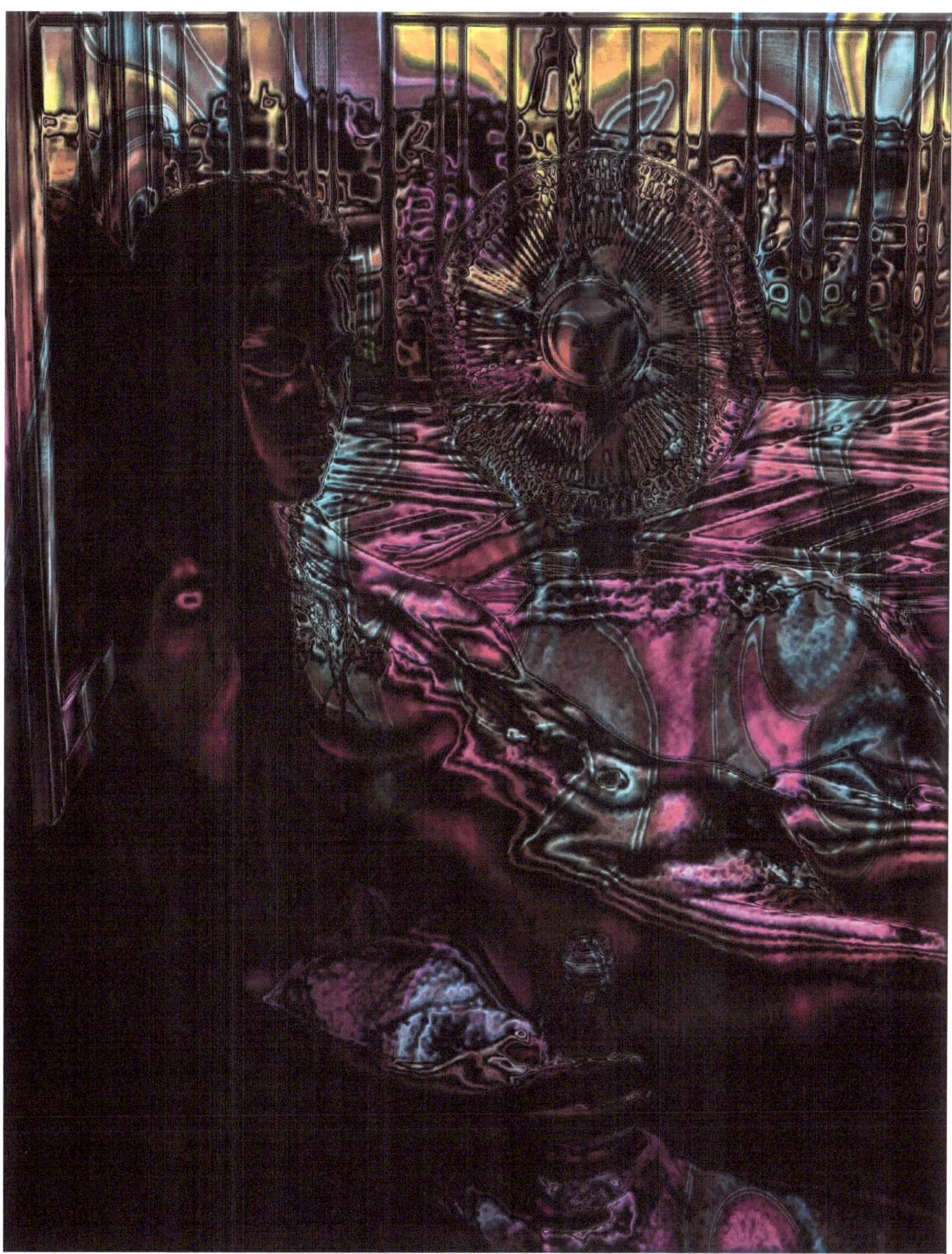

JENNA SATIVA

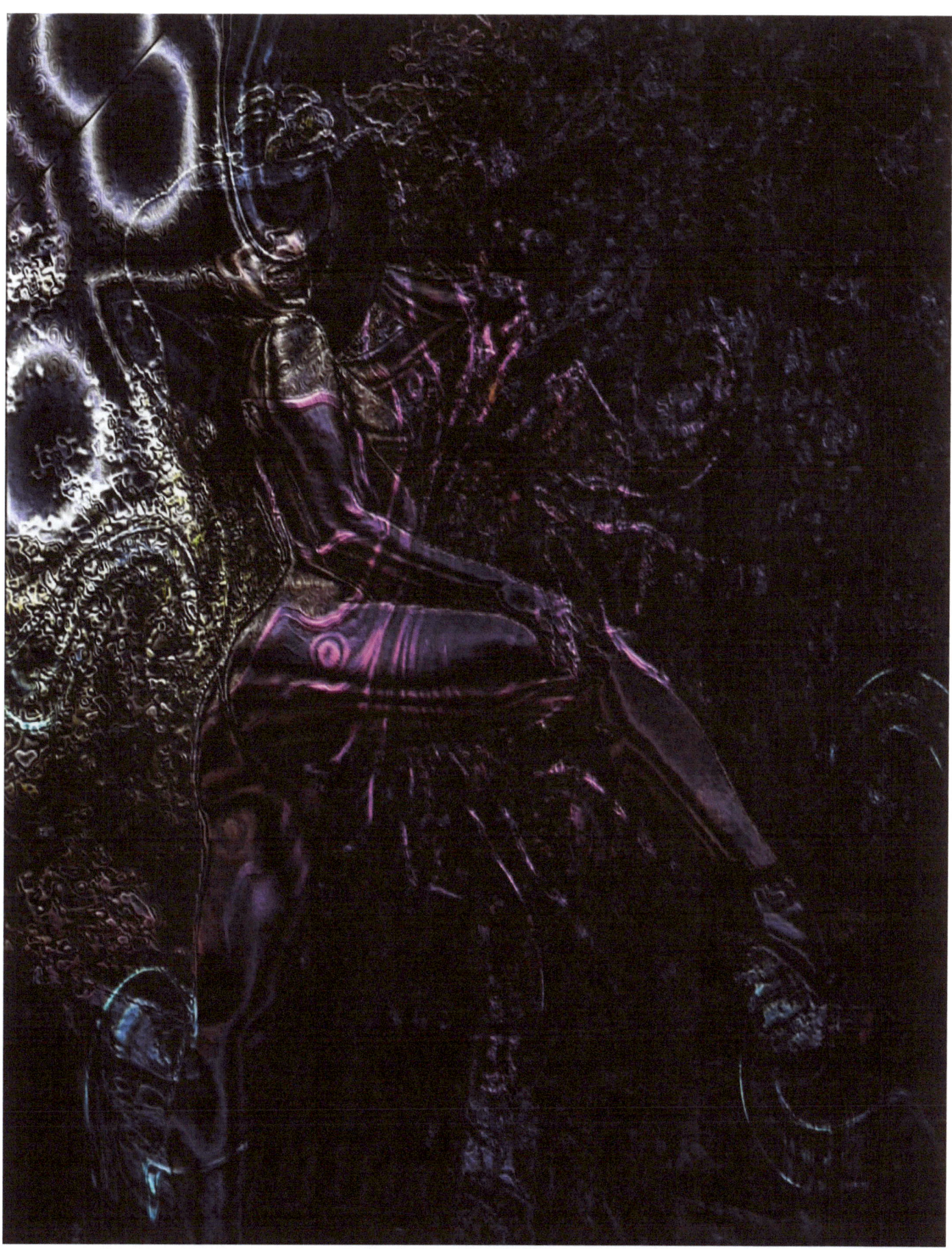

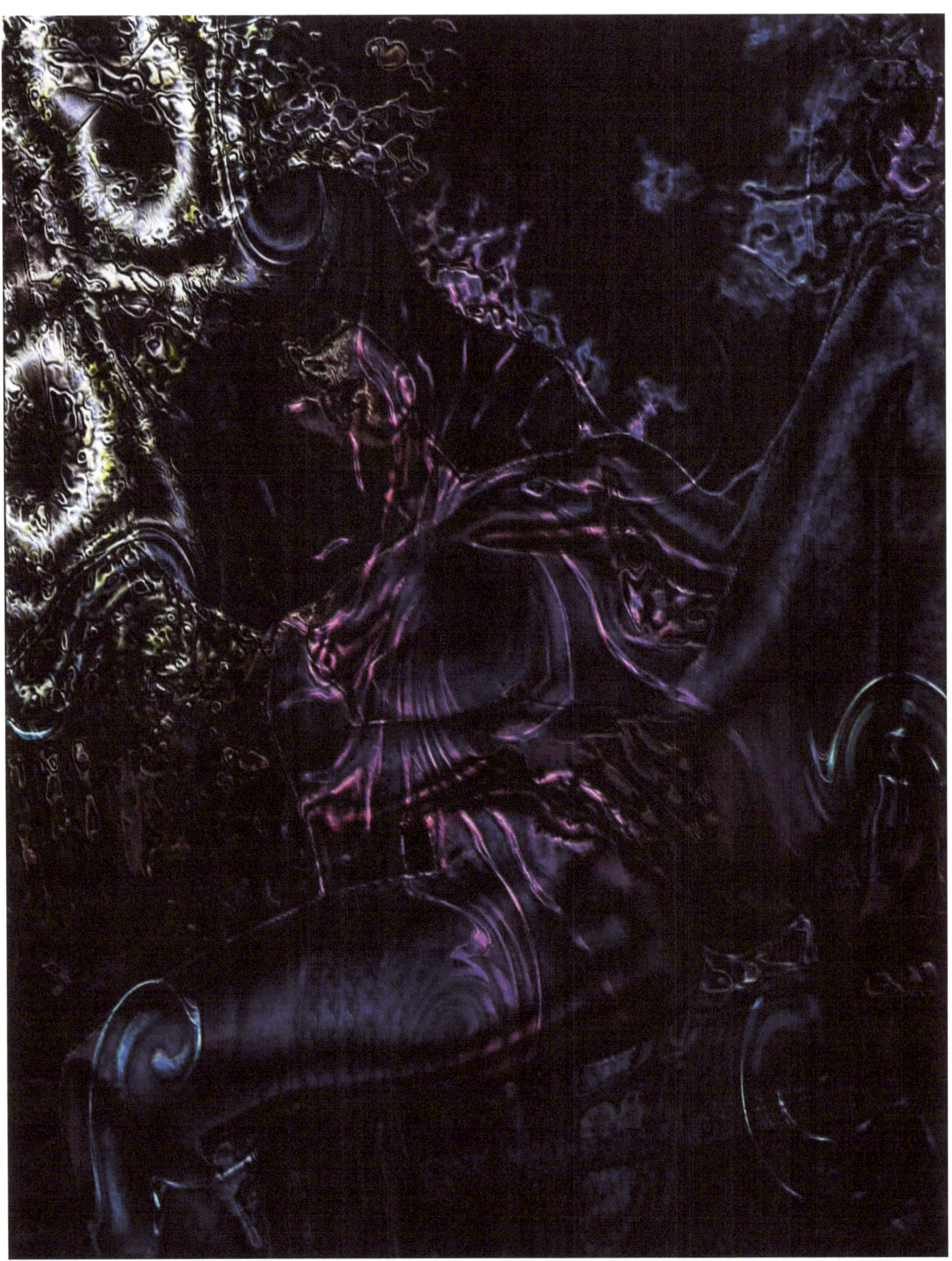

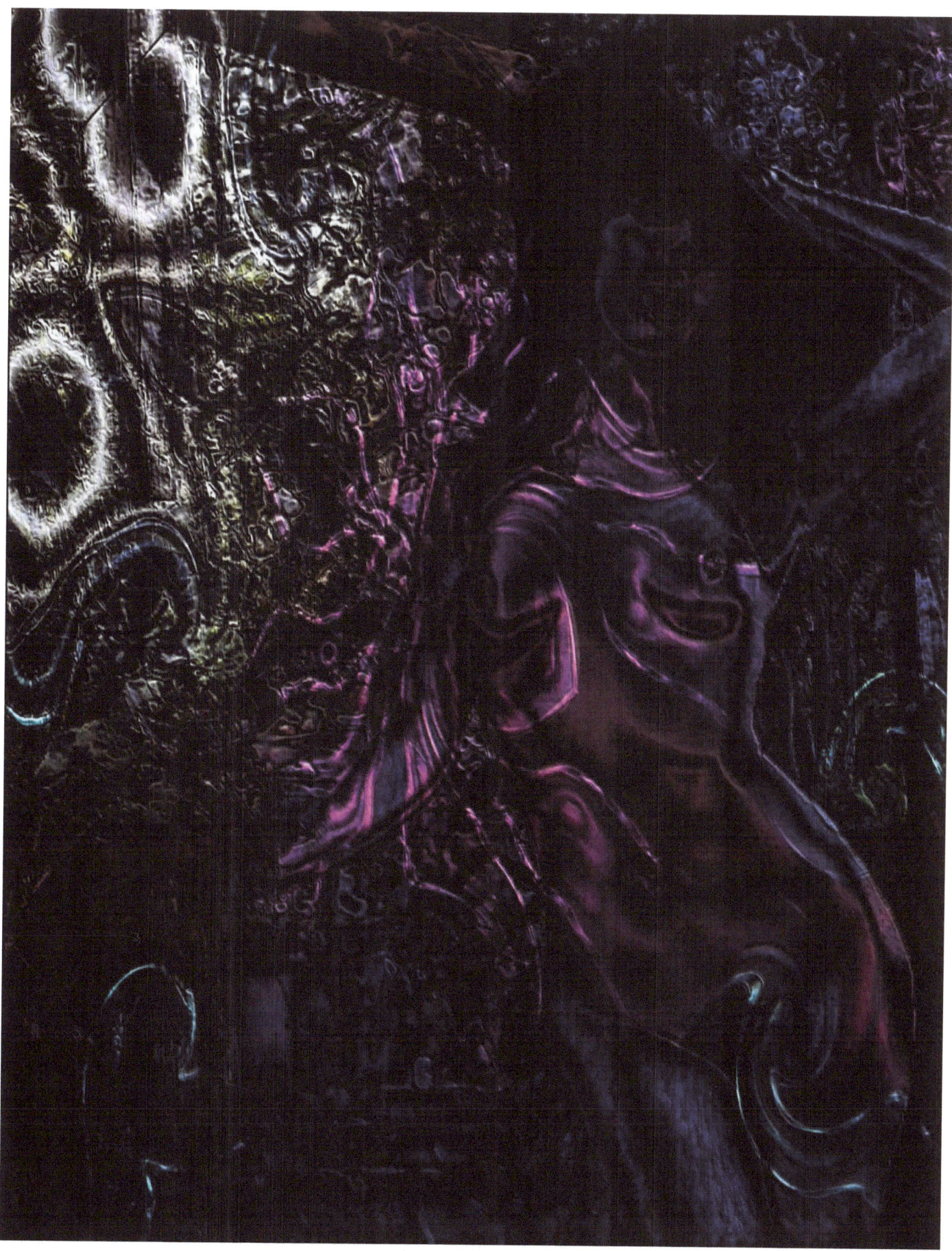

.BLAKE EDEN

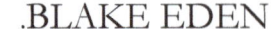

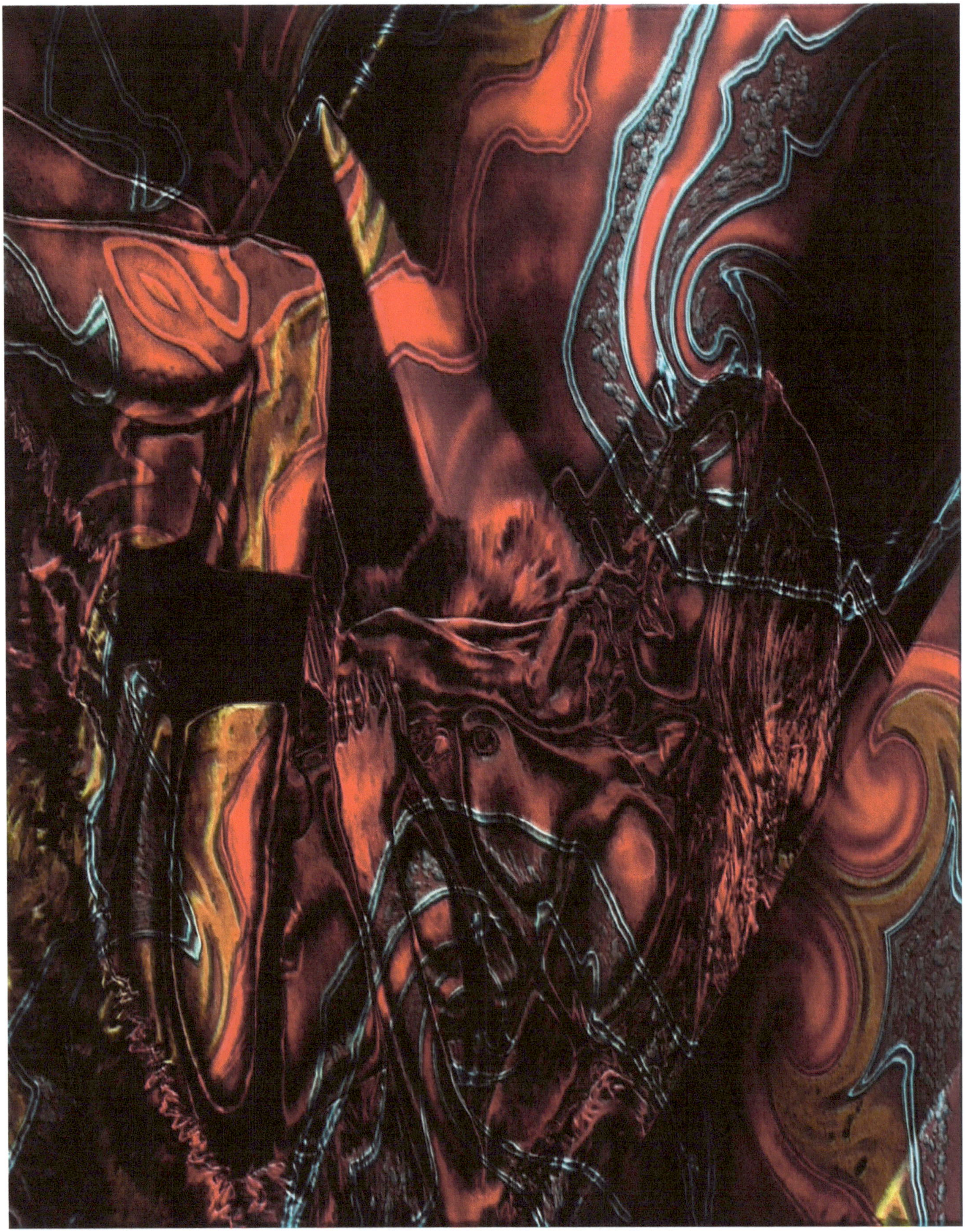

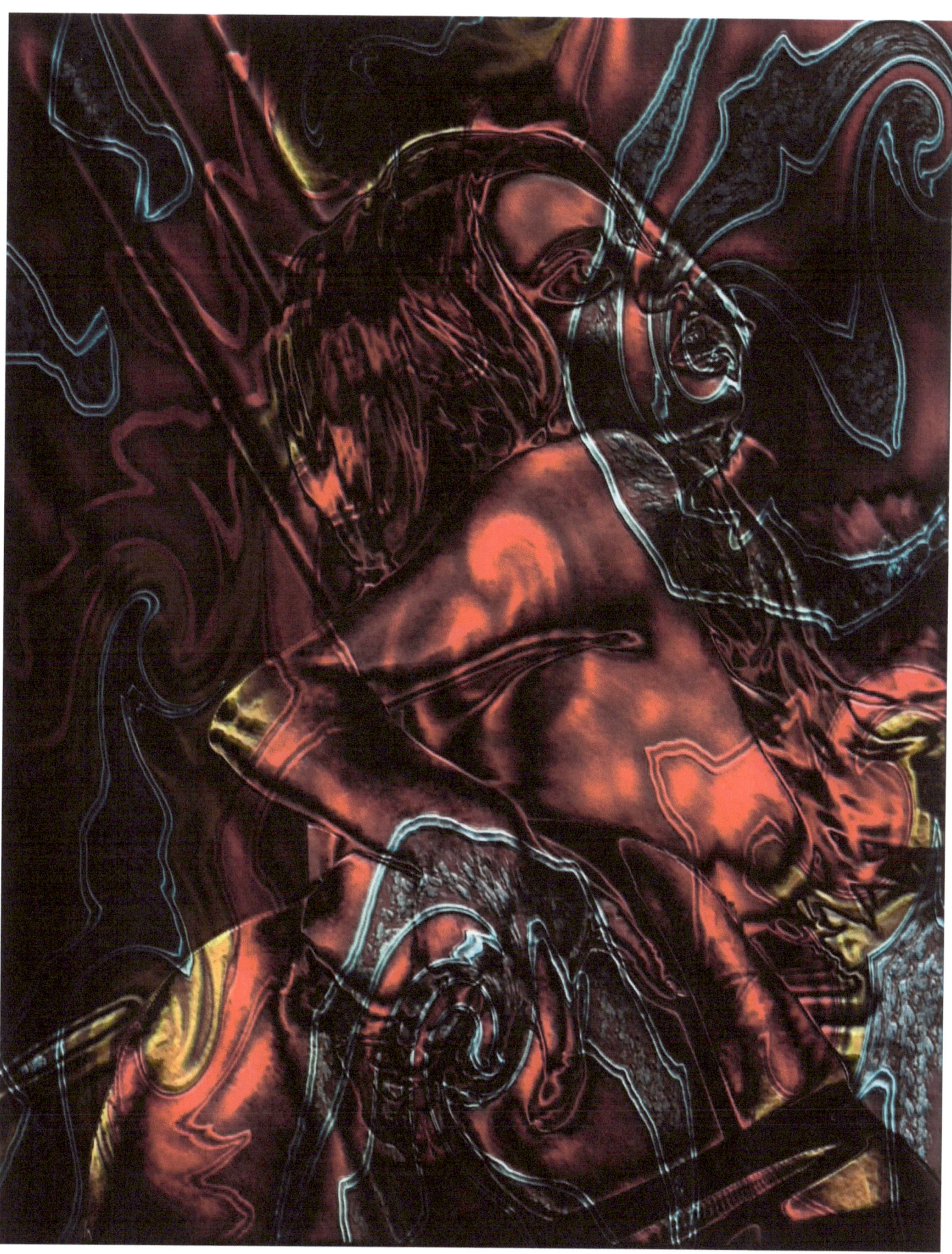

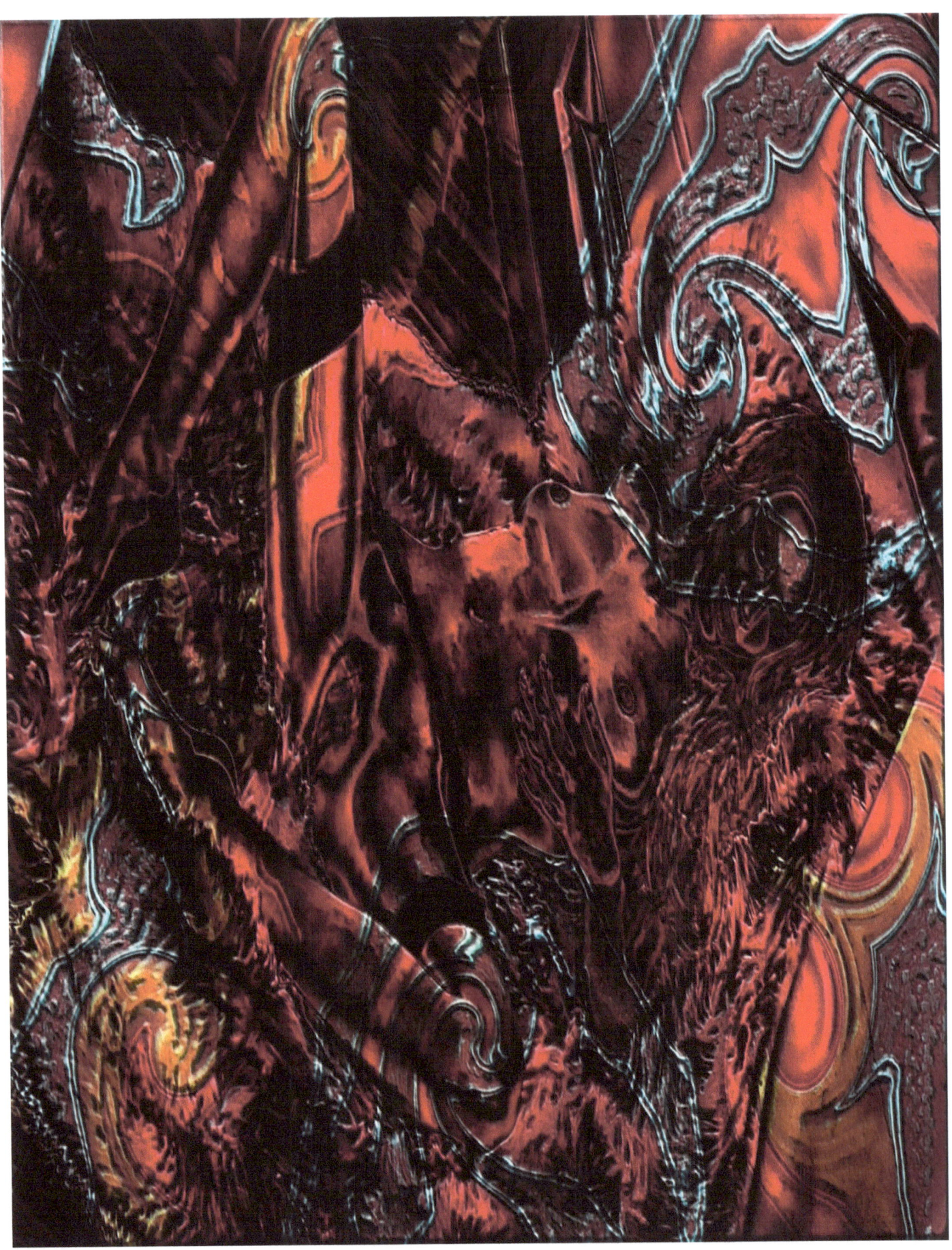

Codex Venereorum Abstracta

DARCIE DOLCE

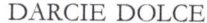

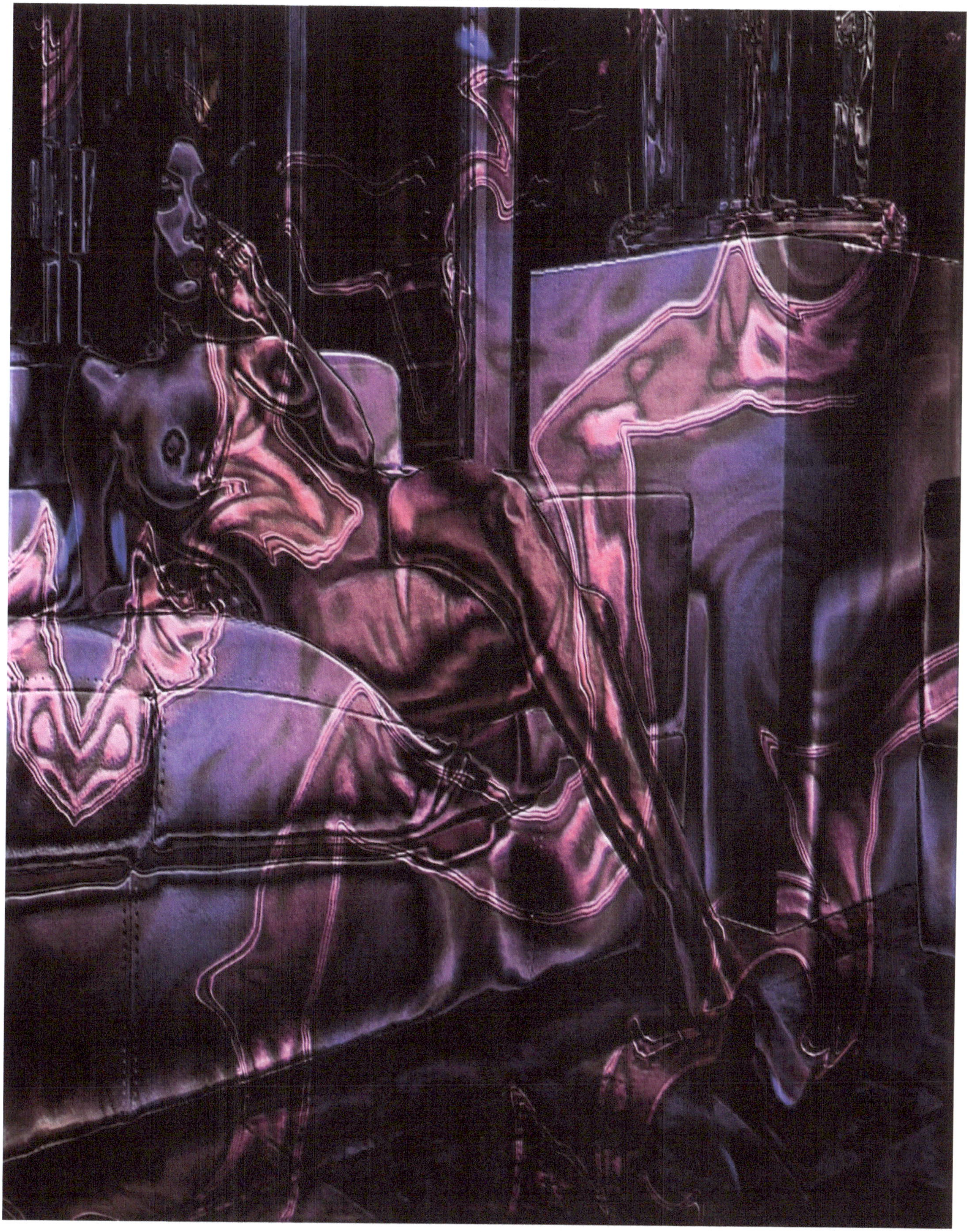

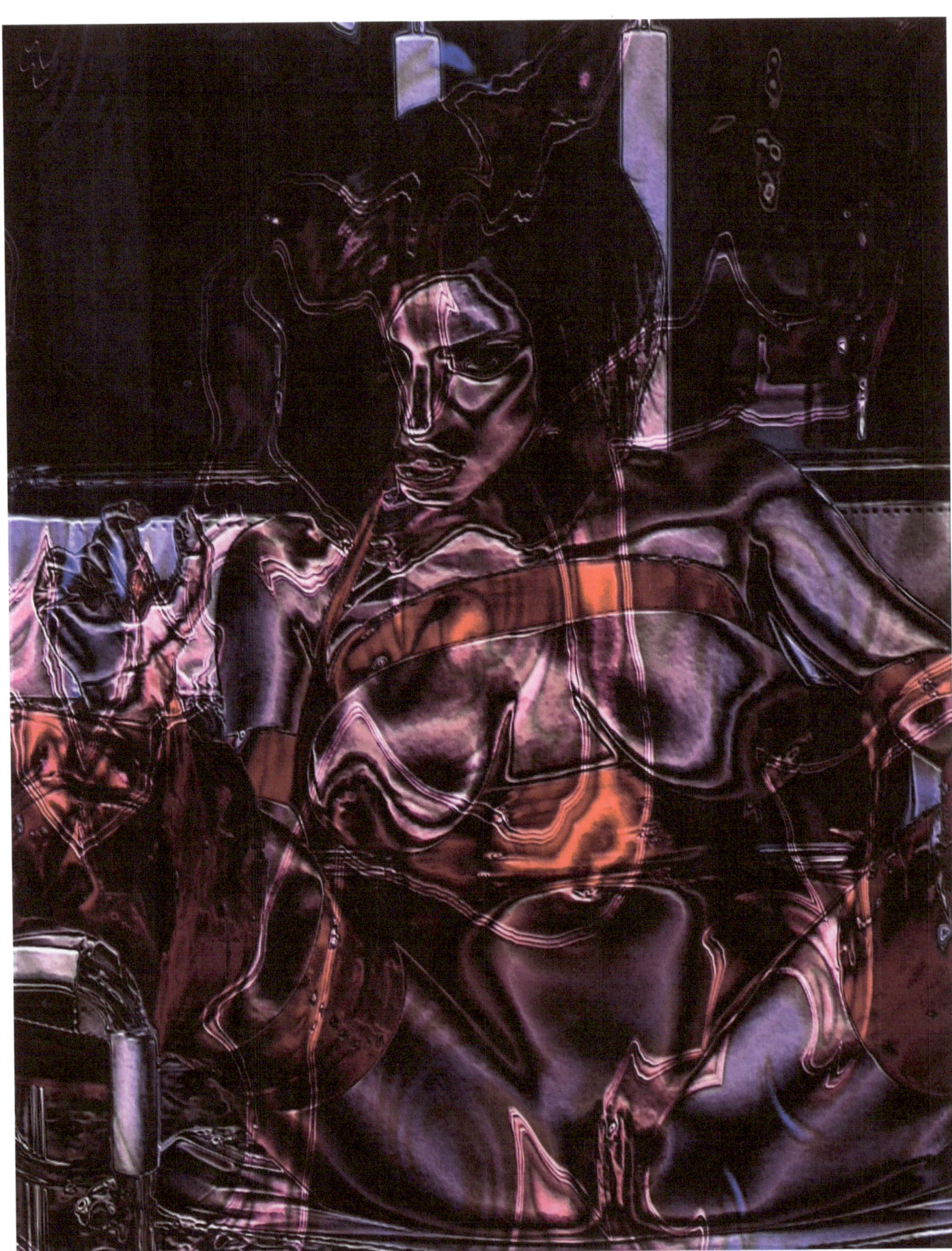

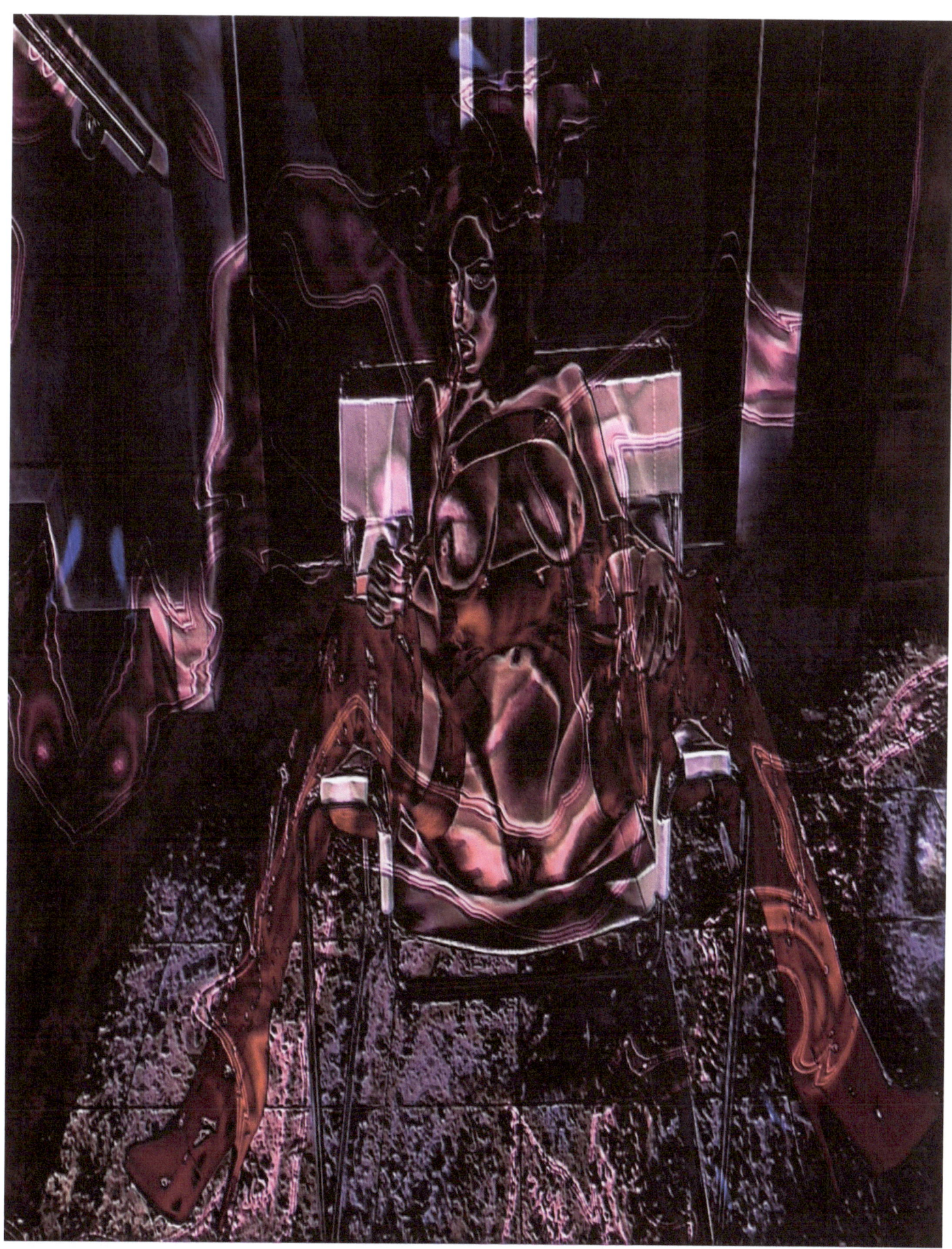

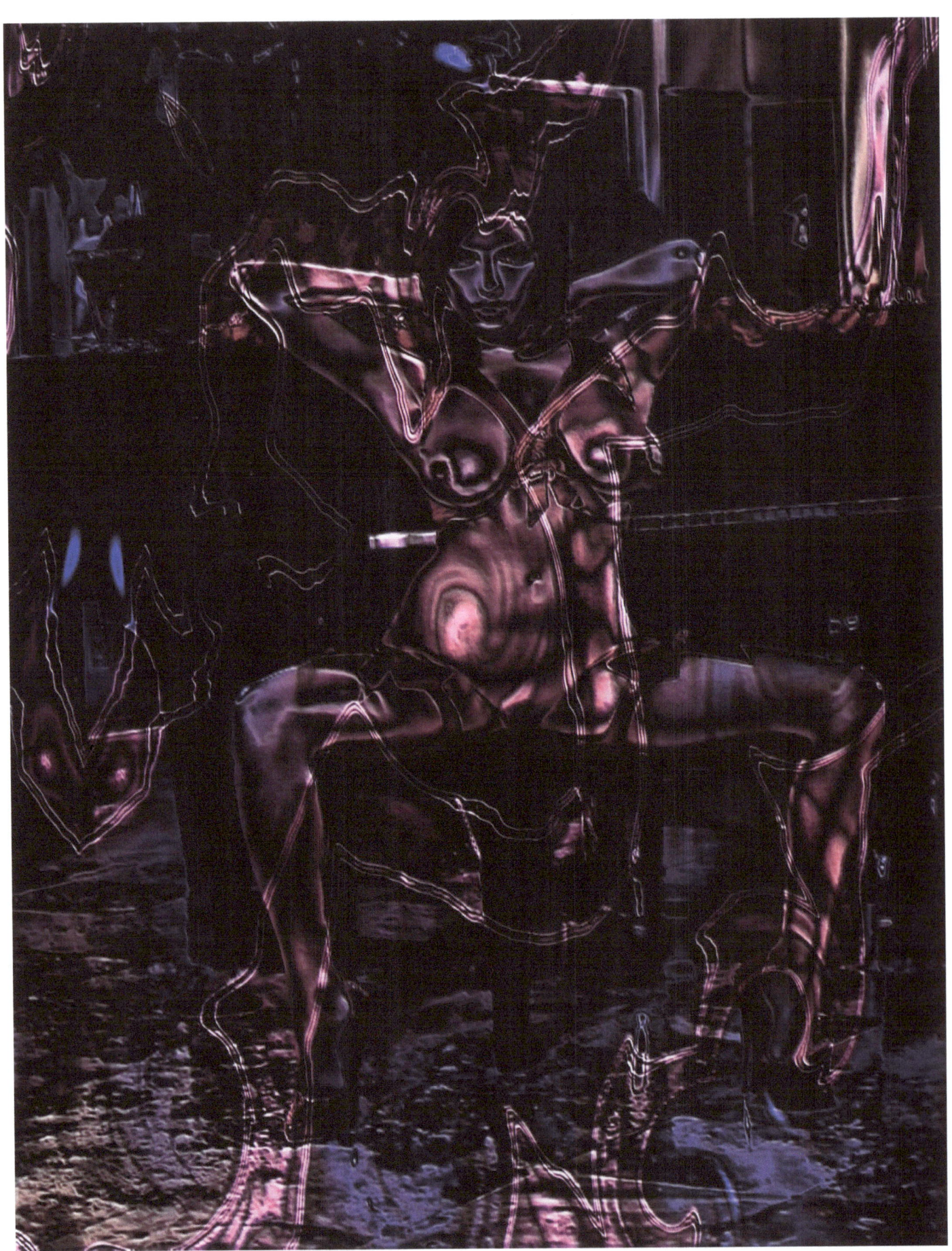

CHRISTIANA CINN

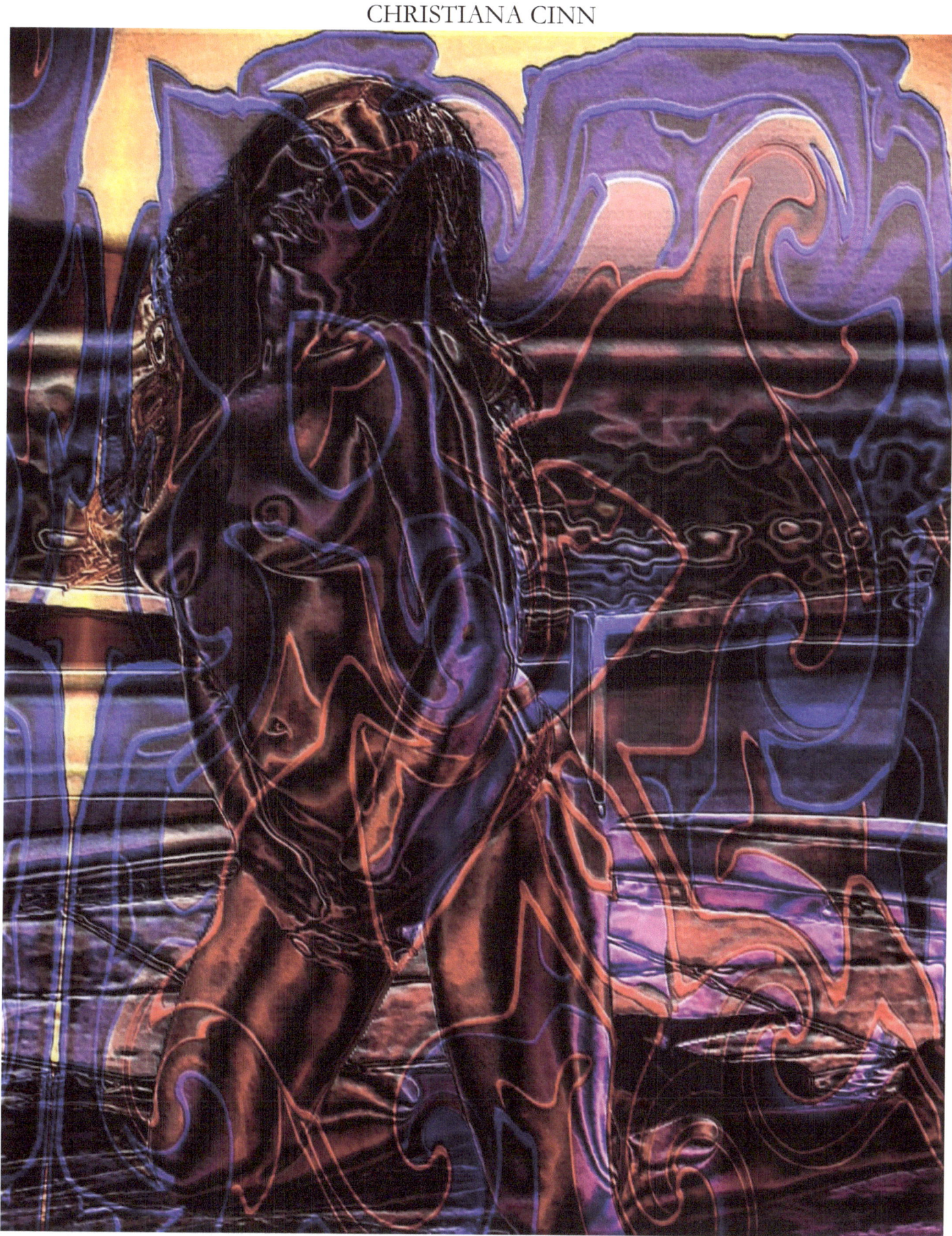

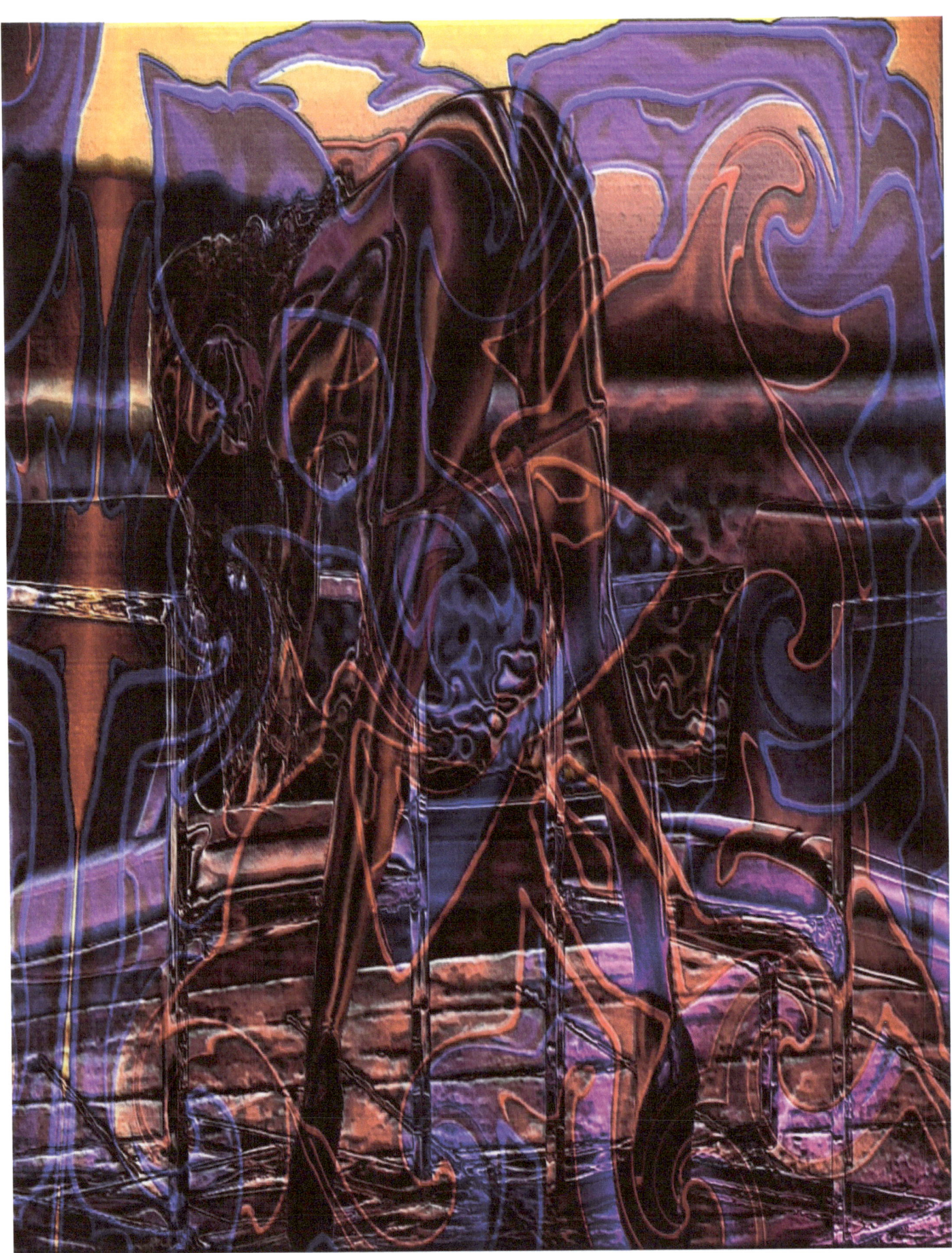

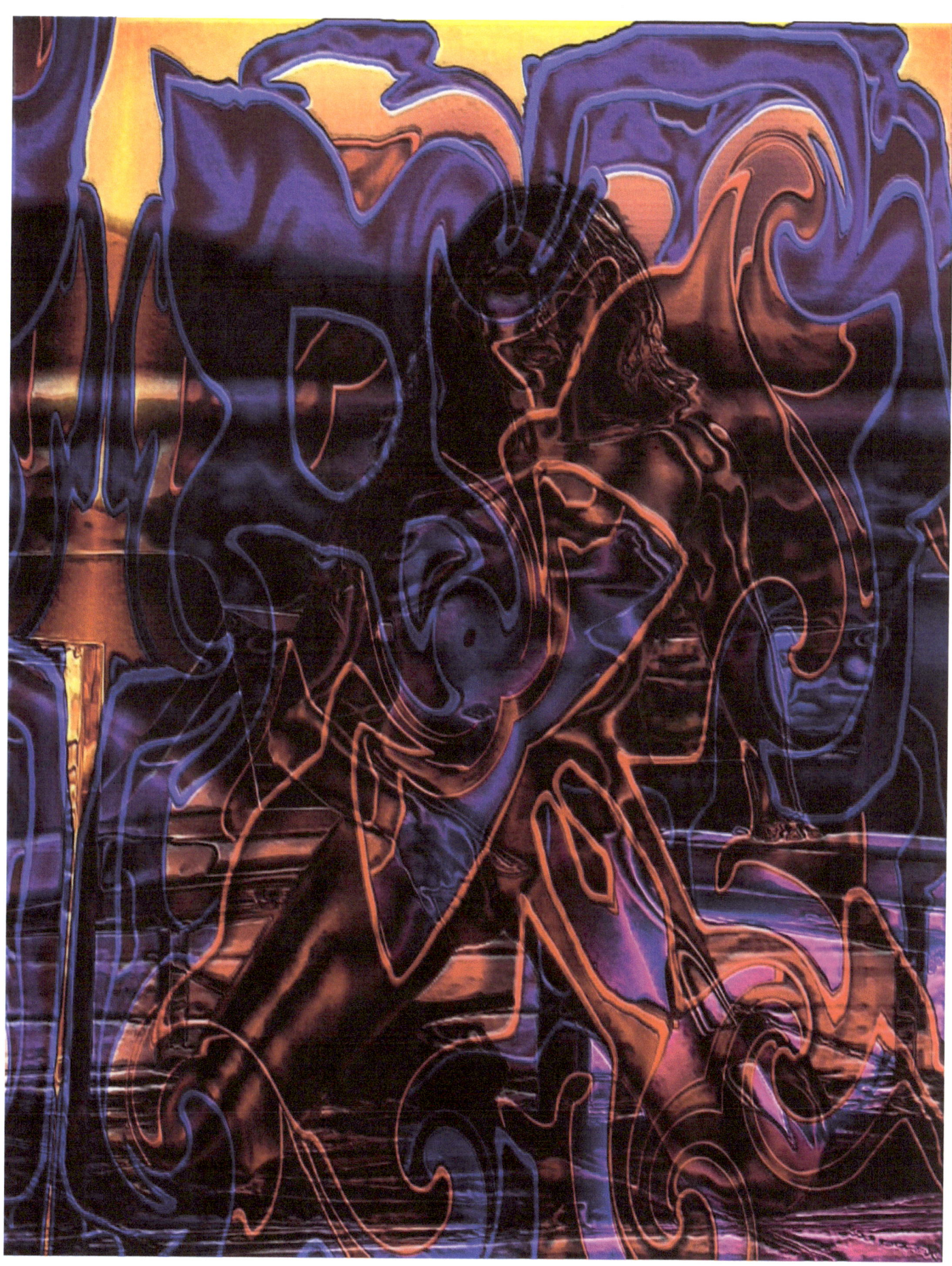

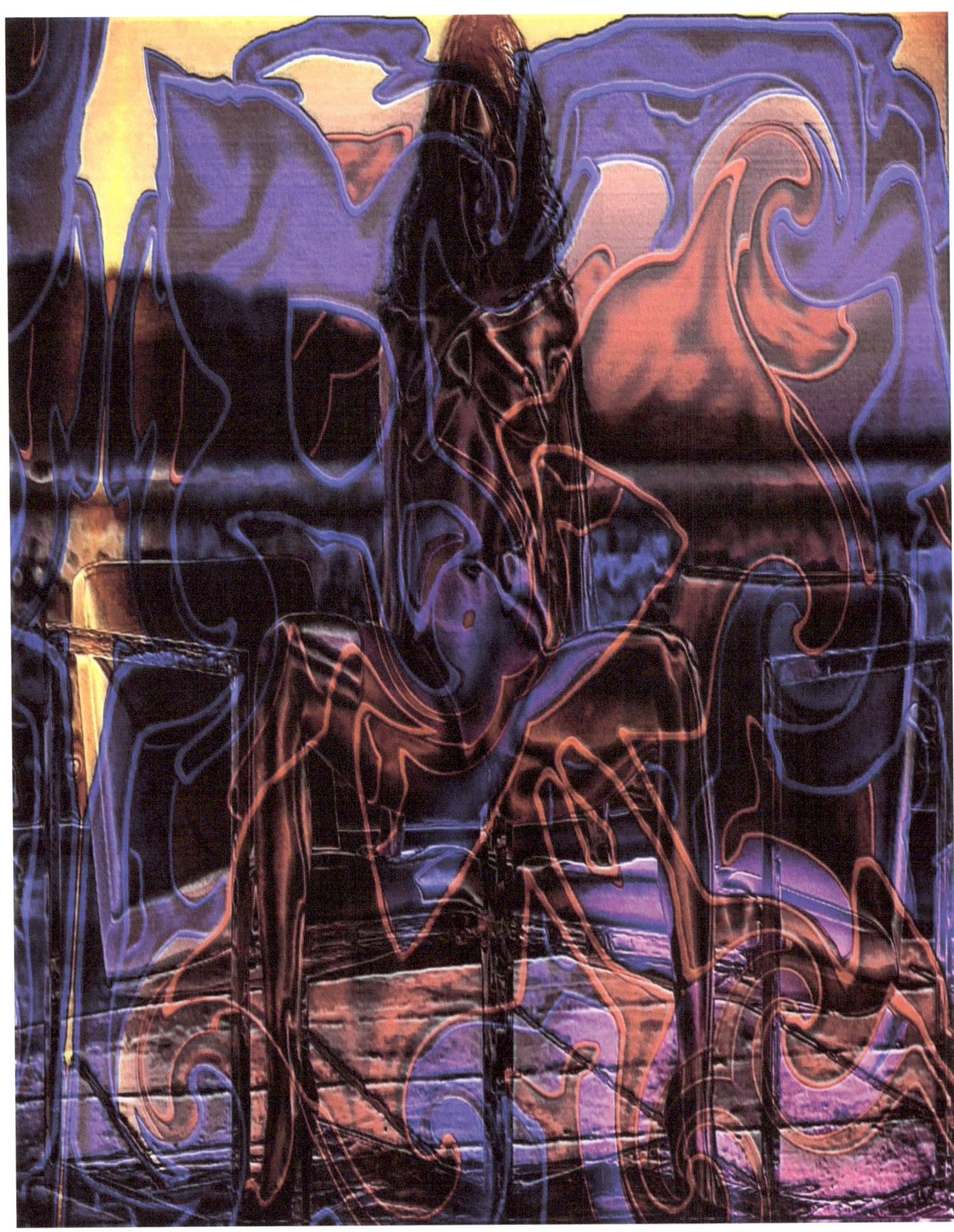

About the author

Mark Humes is a Digital abstract artist and the author of The Book Of Lost Verses series.
To view and purchase the artwork seen in this book as well as all of the author's creations, please visit our website.
http://www.markhumes.gallery

www.ingramcontent.com/pod-product-compliance
Lightning Source LLC
Chambersburg PA
CBHW050813180526
45159CB00004B/1644